SERIOUS
FLAMENCO

~2 AM
VALLADOLID

SURREPTITIOUS STILLMAN
SEVILLA STUDIOS

BOOM CREW

11/1/64

CHARLTON HESTON'S
HOLLYWOOD

50 YEARS IN AMERICAN FILM

BY

CHARLTON HESTON

AND

JEAN-PIERRE ISBOUTS

GT PUBLISHING · NEW YORK

Additional acknowledgments and picture
credits are on page 218.

Published in 1998 by
GT Publishing Corporation
16 East 40th Street
New York, NY 10016

Library of Congress
Cataloging-in-Publication Data
Heston, Charlton.
Charlton Heston's Hollywood: 50 years in
American film / by Charlton Heston and
Jean-Pierre Isbouts.
p.   cm.
Includes bibliographical references and
index.
ISBN 1-57719-357-1 (HARDCOVER)
1. Heston, Charlton. 2. Motion picture actors
and actresses–United States–Biography. I.
Isbouts, Jean-Pierre. II. Title.
PN2287.H47A3 1998
791.43'28'092–dc21
[b]   98-25677
                            CIP

Printed in the United States of America

10 9 8 7 6 5 4 3 2 1

First Printing

Photo captions for front matter, preface,
and chapter openers:

PAGE 1: Lining up a shot in *Antony and
Cleopatra*, 1973.

PAGE 2: Top left: With Yul Brynner in *The
Ten Commandments*, 1956. Top right: In
The Agony and the Ecstasy, 1965. Bottom
left: In *Earthquake*, 1974. Bottom right:
With Janet Leigh in *Touch of Evil*, 1958.

PAGE 16: Sketching in Rome during the
Ben-Hur shoot.

PAGE 10: Top left: With Lydia in
Detective Story, 1957. Top right: With
Anne Bancroft in "Letter to Cairo," 1952.
Bottom left: With Judith Evelyn in
"Macbeth," 1952. Bottom right: My
second try at *Julius Caesar*, 1950.

PAGE 30: Top left: With Betty Hutton in
The Greatest Show on Earth, 1952. Top
right: With Lizabeth Scott in *Dark City*,
1950. Bottom left: With Jack Palance in
Arrowhead, 1953. Bottom right: With
Eleanor Parker in *The Naked Jungle*, 1954.

PAGE 54: Top left: As Moses in *The Ten
Commandments*, 1956. Top right: With
Fraser as the baby Moses. Bottom: With
Yul Brynner as Pharaoh.

PAGE 72: Top left: With Janet Leigh in
Touch of Evil, 1958. Top right: Yours truly.
Bottom: With Carroll Baker and Gregory
Peck in *The Big Country*, 1958.

PAGE 96: Top left: With Lydia and Fraser
in the Roman Forum. Top right: With Jack
Hawkins as Quintas. Bottom: Chariot rides
were the hot ticket in Rome that summer.

PAGE 118: Top left: Typing between
scenes on the set of *Major Dundee*, 1965.
Top right: Riding on to battle in *El Cid*,
1961. Bottom left: General Gordon arrives
in Khartoum, 1966. Bottom right: As
Michelangelo in *The Agony and the
Ecstasy*, 1965.

PAGE 154: Left: As Cardinal Richelieu
in *The Three Musketeers*, 1973.
Center: With Roddy McDowell in *Planet
of the Apes*, 1968. Bottom: In *Antony
and Cleopatra*, 1973.

PAGE 176: Left: With George Kennedy in
Earthquake, 1974. Right: With Karen Black
in *Airport 1975*, 1974. Bottom: With Fraser
on the set of *The Mountain Men*, 1980.

PAGE 88: Left: In *Mother Lode*, 1982.
Right: With President Reagan. Bottom: In
Hamlet, 1996.

CONTENTS

CAMERA
PINEWOOD '65
Heston

PREFACE

THE PROBLEM WITH MANY Hollywood biographies is that they tend to treat their subject in isolation. Biographers, naturally, want to create as complete a picture of their subjects as possible, but they often lose sight of the fact that actors and actresses, like the rest of us, are a product of their time—and the unique set of circumstances that brought them success.

Charlton Heston's career is no exception. While the sheer breadth of his work is truly impressive—seventy-five films over a time span of fifty years—even more remarkable is the fact that his story is, in many ways, the story of Hollywood. By fortuitous circumstance, Heston found himself, time and again, at pivotal moments in the history of postwar entertainment. He was a rising star in the early days of live television, then emerged as the epic hero of Hollywood's big-screen historical dramas, designed to thwart the growing competition from television. Already the star of two DeMille features, he was one of the first Hollywood actors to throw his support behind the civil-rights protests of the early 1960s. When the public tired of costume epics, Hollywood shifted gears in favor of contemporary adventures, and Heston effortlessly migrated to the role of a modern action hero. His starring role in *Planet of the Apes* (1968) helped launch the revival of the science-fiction film, a genre that continues to thrill audiences to this day. *Earthquake* (1974) was one of the first of countless disaster movies that pulled Hollywood out of its doldrums in the 1970s. His remake of *A Man for All Seasons* (1988) was one of the first films made for premium cable, at a time when much of Hollywood considered cable television hopelessly *déclassé*. Intrigued with the possibility of multimedia, he hosted two interactive CD-ROMs, and continues to straddle the worlds of television, feature films, and the stage to this day.

Heston's influence was also felt behind the scenes of Hollywood. He was a six-term president of the Screen Actors Guild at a time when the relationship among Hollywood actors, studios, and producers went through a period of profound change. As chairman of the American Film Institute, he became a staunch defender of American film culture and the film preservation movement. Between jobs, he was called upon by both Democratic and Republican administrations to embark on missions of goodwill to Third World nations around the globe. He twice traveled to Vietnam and came closer to combat than any Hollywood actor or actress ever has. During the Reagan administration's campaign to curb government spending on certain federal programs, Heston was called upon to render judgment on the National Endowment for the Arts, and surprised much of Washington by staunchly defending it. Quite possibly, he is the only major Hollywood actor to have had full security clearance without ever having served in office.

Heston's career, both on-camera and off, is not only the story of Charlton Heston; it is the story of Hollywood and a turbulent time in modern American history. In his own 1995 autobiography, *In the Arena*, a title taken from a speech by Teddy Roosevelt, one of Heston's favorite Americans, "Chuck" Heston is modest about his role in Hollywood history. *Charlton Heston's Hollywood* attempts to illustrate his greater role in Hollywood, both in text and pictures, including many unpublished photographs taken by his wife, Lydia Clarke Heston, and his own sketches drawn on the sets of many of his movies.

In his personal life, Heston hardly fits the role of a Hollywood megastar. As he confided to his journals, published in 1976 as *An Actor's Life*, he is an intensely private man who doesn't make friends easily. "Some time ago," he said, "someone pointed out how often I play withdrawn, alienated men. There is some truth in that. The real historical characters that I've played, like General Charles Gordon, Andrew Jackson, Thomas Jefferson, John the Baptist, El Cid, Moses, didn't lead very happy lives. Most of these guys were too busy inventing the United States or painting the Sistine Ceiling or driving the Moors out of Spain to have many laughs. Did I acquire this from the parts, or did I bring this to the parts? It is an interesting question."

The art of Charlton Heston may have spanned a broad range of characters, but it is firmly rooted in the plays of William Shakespeare, which opened Heston's eyes to the stage when he was just starting out as an actor. Throughout his career, he has never passed up an opportunity to "waltz with the old gentleman," as he puts it. Playing Shakespeare, or Shaw or O'Neill for that matter, has always enabled him to recharge his batteries, particularly when his work in motion pictures sometimes left him looking for a creative challenge. Sir Laurence Olivier, one of his idols, called Heston "quite possibly the greatest American Shakespearean actor." In redacting the Shakespeare text of *Antony and Cleopatra*—or the nearly contemporary King James Bible text for his A&E mini-series on the Bible—Chuck found perhaps his greatest source of joy and fulfillment. Unquestionably, these classical roots have endeared him to British fans and critics alike, as much, or perhaps even more so, than to fans in the country of his birth. It is no accident that of the three biographies published about Heston to date, two were written by British authors.

I am indebted to John Stronach, who first proposed the concept of this book and who has been invaluable as a catalyst in our many discussions as well as in reviewing drafts of the manuscript. Lydia Heston added her recollections to those of Chuck, and contributed a treasure trove of behind-the-scenes photographs, shot from the very beginning of Chuck's Hollywood career. I am most grateful to our researchers, Misty Perry and Benita Heet, who worked long hours at the Academy of Motion Picture Arts and Sciences, and to the Academy staff, particularly Faye Thompson, Robert Cushman, Grafton Harper, and Linda Harris Mehr, who ably assisted them in their research. I am equally indebted to the staff at the UCLA Research Library. Leslie Stoker at GoodTimes Publishing was unwavering in her support. A heartfelt thanks is due to our editor, Ruth Greenstein, whose keen eye greatly strengthened the manuscript. Cathie Labrador, who became my wife in the course of this project, was a constant source of kind scrutiny and guidance.

JEAN-PIERRE ISBOUTS, April 1998

From Broadway

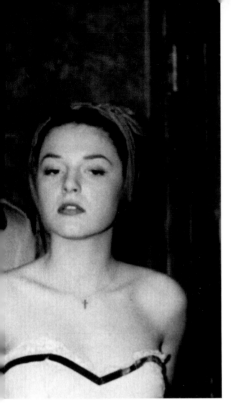

More or less by default, this new entertainment medium was left in the hands of a bunch of unemployed 24-year-olds— including, fortunately, me.

to TELEVISION

1947 WAS THE KIND OF YEAR
historians rarely write about but everyone remembers. There was no public scandal, no market crash, no floods in the Midwest. The long victory party in celebration of the end of World War II and the defeat of the Axis powers was over; the Cold War with the Soviets still lay in the future. Now it was time to adjust to peace.

The first problem was what to do with the GIs. All of a sudden, the nation was flooded by 13 million young Americans whose education had been interrupted, who needed shelter, and who for the last five years had learned nothing better than bombing cities or lobbing grenades. Among them was a twenty-three-year-old student from Northwestern University whose name was Charlton Heston.

Heston had joined the Army Air Corps in 1942 and, after basic training and a few months at several stateside air bases, spent the last two years of his military service on the Aleutian Islands, dispatched there after Army Intelligence had reported renewed Japanese activity around the islands. By the time Sergeant Heston arrived there in mid-1944 to join the 11th Air Force, though, it was clear that Japan was too busy defending its territory to worry about new invasions.

We rarely flew and were seldom in harm's way, unless you take the weather into account. The average wind velocity in the Aleutians is thirty-two miles per hour; if you go down in the Northern Pacific, your survival time in the water is six minutes.

However, every man in the Pacific Theater dreaded the next phase in the war: the invasion of Japan. Unquestionably, that enterprise would be the bloodiest, most costly military campaign in American history. It was estimated that casualties could mount to as many as half a million American soldiers. It was not a prospect anyone was looking forward to—least of all the young soldier from Michigan, who was counting the days before he could return to the arms of his college sweetheart, Lydia Clarke.

HE WAS BORN ON October 4, 1924 in a tiny house on Lake Michigan, in one of Chicago's northern suburbs, and given his mother Lilla's maiden name, which was Charlton. Lilla hailed from Scots/English stock, and had married Russell Whitford Carter, who operated a lumber mill in St. Helen, Michigan.

My father was a good-looking man of immense charm, with a rich bass voice. The voice was perhaps his most useful bequest to me. It has gotten me a lot of parts.

I grew up in St. Helen, a very remote part of Michigan. It was a marvelous childhood. The forests of Michigan were a wonderful place for a boy to grow up, even though it was a bit lonely. There weren't any kids my age I could play with; I was simply left to my own devices most of the time.

I used to read books, and then I went outside to act out the stories—just me, playing all the parts. If anything, that's what probably got me started in acting. For a young boy, acting is a pretend game. I pretended I was the characters of all the books I read, and no doubt it planted the seeds of my career.

When Chuck was nine, Russ and Lilla decided to divorce. In due course, Lilla married a man named Chester Heston, and soon after that the new family left St. Helen, with a trailer full of belongings towed behind the car. It was the height of the Depression, and Chet couldn't find work. The Heston family moved from one town to the next, in pursuit of the rumor of "plenty of jobs." Finally, they settled in Wilmette, a suburb north of Chicago not far from the place where Chuck had been born.

Chuck went to what was regarded as the best public high school in the country, New Trier High

School, in nearby Winnetka. He grew rapidly, reaching a height of six feet two inches by the age of sixteen. He also found something in school that appealed to his vivid imagination: New Trier's drama classes: *I realized that my youthful game of pretend was actually something that adults did too, on stage. Mind you, you could even take classes in it.* One day, he went to see a play called *Twelfth Night*. Right then and there, he decided that this is what he wanted to do for the rest of his life: pretend to be someone else—to *act*. Before long, Chuck appeared in a number of school plays as well in the productions of the nearby Winnetka Drama Club. He also came to the attention of a young amateur filmmaker by the name of David Bradley. Bradley was planning to make a silent 16mm film of Ibsen's play *Peer Gynt*. The young director thought that in Heston he had just the right actor to play the title role.

All the actors were amateurs, kids really. We shot it on the shores of Lake Michigan and in Wisconsin. The interiors were shot in the house of David's parents. Why they allowed us to do that I cannot imagine. Having no synchronous sound, Bradley used music by Grieg to emphasize the story—the Peer Gynt Suite, *of course. Very cleverly scored and selected, it was really one of the best parts of the film. The picture could*

Opposite: A very green soldier about to go overseas, 1944. Above: A pensive young soldier. What's that on my upper lip? Right: In the Aleutian Islands, 1944.

only be shown with David Bradley playing the cues, which naturally made the distribution of the film somewhat limited.

In 1965, Bradley produced a revised version of the film in which he featured narration by Francis Bushman. The new *Peer Gynt* gained a following at film festivals and drew fresh accolades from the critics.

After his graduation from high school in 1941, Heston entered Northwestern University's School of Speech on a scholarship from the Winnetka Drama Club. There, Chuck plunged into his studies with a fervor matched only by his tireless energy when it came to making ends meet. He mowed lawns, and even took a night job as an elevator operator in an apartment building: *Now, you won't believe me, but that's a job I can heartily recommend to anyone. You have the whole lobby to yourself to rehearse your acting, and when you're tired you simply doze off for a while.*

There was one other thing that occupied Heston's time: how to approach an attractive young speech school student with whom, he realized, he had fallen in love. Her name was Lydia Clarke, and she had been born in a town called Two Rivers, Wisconsin: *Lydia's first impression of me,*

Above: As a senior at New Trier High School, I was cast in the title role of *Peer Gynt*, my first film. Right: At age 16 in David Bradley's film *Peer Gynt*, 1940. Opposite: Shooting on the shores of Lake Michigan.

Above and opposite: Lydia as a student and a model. Can you believe she's even more beautiful today?

most likely, was that I was the most incredible creature in the school. In the end, I didn't have to muster the courage to talk to her. Fortunately, she came to me.

Lydia was rehearsing a new role in a play and turned to Chuck for advice on her reading. Young Heston rose to the occasion and, after a successful opening night, asked her out for some coffee.

Of course, as we walked off-campus to the coffee shop, I realized that I had no money. Not a nickel. I certainly couldn't mention this to the celestial beauty actually walking beside me; all I could do was silently pray that there would be a pal in the coffee shop that I could hit on for a loan. Fortunately, there was—and Lydia and I had tea, which lasts longer, because you can get more hot water for free. I was head over heels in love with her, but I've never quite understood what drew her to me. Lydia has never been very forthcoming on the question. When I pressed her on this subject once, she merely smiled and said, "Words, Charlie . . . words. I loved the way you talked about things."

They began to date—or what passed for it. "He took me for a long romantic walk," Lydia later recalled, "but instead of taking me into his arms and kissing me, he sat me down and read long passages from *Macbeth!* I figured we would get around to the romantic part later." Still, these nocturnal readings had their effect. Before

long, Lydia switched her major from law to drama. Chuck was almost too smitten to notice that the country was at war—which it very much was since Japan's attack on Pearl Harbor on December 7, 1941. "I enlisted in the Army Air Corps because it seemed more gallant than the regular Army," Heston later wrote, "even though I hadn't been near an airplane since my first glimpse of a fabric biplane in a Michigan pasture."

When the day of his call-up came near, Heston besieged his girl to marry him. She said no; she thought it best to finish her studies first.

I then fell back on the ploy that soldiers have used for centuries: "But you realize you may never see me again. We must have something to carry in our hearts! It may be years, it may be never." I gave her a heartbreaking performance, not least because I meant it, but it never dented her resolve. She was not going to marry anybody, and she was not going to bed with me.

Heston was called to the colors still a bachelor, and off he went. From his training camp in Greensboro, North Carolina, he wrote long letters. Then one day, he returned from a fun day on the rifle range to find a telegram on his bunk. It said, "HAVE DECIDED TO ACCEPT YOUR PROPOSAL. LOVE, LYDIA." On March 17, 1944, she came down to Greensboro. Heston equipped himself with a two-day pass and two twelve-dollar rings, pressed two elderly ladies into service as witnesses, and married his girl in Greensboro's small Methodist church.

In August 1945, President Harry Truman made a difficult decision that would have a profound effect on Sergeant Heston and the millions of other young Americans fighting the war in the Pacific. In response to his order, a B-29 bomber lifted off from Tinian Island in the Marianas and set course for mainland Japan. Approaching the thriving provincial capital of Hiroshima, the bombardier dropped the only bomb the plane carried. That done, the pilot executed a sharp turn and set course for the home base, while behind him 80,000 people died in a man-made nuclear holocaust. Two days later, the city of Nagasaki underwent the same fate, and the prospect of a long and bloody war on Japanese soil was eliminated.

Seven months after that, Charlton Heston was at long last reunited with his wife, almost two years to the day since he had last held her in his arms. The first days of their reunion sped by in a sweet cloud of new-found marital bliss. Then one day, he woke up and realized that it was time to decide what to do next.

There was the GI Bill, of course, which made a return to college very attractive. Heston decided it was time to put his acting ability to the test.

Of course, finding a decent place to live was out of the question what with the housing shortage. Luckily, Lydia still had a one-room studio in Chicago. It became the headquarters from which the two of them set out in search of an acting career—and found out, to their dismay, that their timing could not have been worse. Since

1946, the cost of living had risen by 23 percent, and food prices by 40 percent. Chuck was getting $20 a week as veteran's pay; Lydia was making a bit more as a model. It didn't add up to a whole lot.

The cost spiral was affecting the entire nation, even Hollywood. The film business suffered as ticket prices for new releases rose to $1.80, and in some New York theaters, to as much as $2.40 on weekends. For the first time, an average Joe who wanted to take his wife and two kids to the movies had to spend $10 just on tickets—an enormous sum, when the average monthly salary was $350.

Broadway was doing poorly as well. The cost of new productions had skyrocketed, many shows now costing twice as much as they had only five years ago. As a result, theater funding dried up as many investors got cold feet. Broadway responded the way Broadway has always responded in times of crisis: it staged revivals, and shelved its new and risky productions. One director, Harry Wagstaff Gribble, floated the idea to stage William Shakespeare's *Romeo and Juliet*, casting the Capulets with all-black performers and the Montagues with all-white actors. It was a crazy idea, but then again, Gribble (a British director) had already had a hit show in Chicago when he staged *Anna Lucasta*, about a family of Polish Jews, with an all-black cast.

While Gribble was in Chicago, he figured he could start casting for Romeo and Juliet, *and I was cast as Mercutio. I must tell you, I was stunned. It's a marvelous part, with one great set-piece speech, which you usually play as a drunk scene. Then there is the quarrel leading to the fight, in which you're killed. Simply wonderful. To make your Broadway debut in a part like Mercutio is the stuff of actors' dreams. To be fair, I was not quite unprepared for the role; I had worked on the part at Northwestern and even at New Trier—and I knew how to fence.*

The rehearsals started and we were essentially waiting for Lucasta *to close before we headed for New York, since much of the* Lucasta *cast also appeared in* Romeo. *Then one day we walked in and were told that the whole thing was off. Either the bankers got cold feet or went bankrupt or decided to do something else with their money, but the bottom line was: they pulled the rug from under us.*

I can't help but wonder what would have happened if we had been able to stage it. Not many years later, Lenny Bernstein hit on essentially the same idea —casting his Capulets as Puerto Ricans against white Montagues to exploit the racial tension between the two. Perhaps America wasn't quite ready for such a play in the late Forties. But what if it had become a huge hit, as West Side Story *did twelve years later? Where would my career have taken me then?*

In any case, there we were, all set and ready to move to New York, and no place to go. What the heck, we said. Let's go anyway. And so we did.

HELL'S KITCHEN, IT WAS CALLED. *The area between Ninth and Eleventh avenues, cold and blustery in winter, scorching hot in summer. Rather trendy now, it was then mostly cold-water walk-up tenements. A quirky but patriotic old Tammany pal who owned several of them decided to "refurbish" one building by painting every flat and installing a small bathroom with running water. The thing was, he would rent it only to overseas veterans. For that, I qualified. Bingo! We had our apartment, albeit four flights up, no heat and no hot water. But at least we were in the Big Apple. The only thing we needed now was an acting job. Aye, there's the rub. It is an axiom in acting, as in just about every other profession I guess, that getting the first part is the hardest. Statistically, it's impossible.*

Fortunately, Lydia soon found work modeling lingerie for the Sunday papers. Acting jobs were scarce—so much so that Heston found himself modeling as well, though not in lingerie. He posed for young artists at the Art Students League, wearing only a jockstrap, which Lydia covered in velvet for him: *Free tea, cookies, and $1.50 an hour. It was fairly tough to hold a pose for a long time, and also quite boring. To pass the time, I used to run Shakespeare soliloquies in my head.*

The weeks went by. Weeks of endless rounds and auditions—*Thank you, just leave your picture.* The result was nil: *To beat the odds, you need the guts of a burglar and skin thick enough to turn cold steel, or at least the cold eye of a casting director.* The only offer that did come through for Heston was the role of an ambulance driver, with five lines. It was the last straw.

A few weeks later, the Hestons were on the road in a Trailways bus, heading for Asheville, North Carolina. Here they stayed for six months, having accepted a generous offer to run the Asheville Community Theater. It was a pretty place: fresh air, simple, courteous folks, and the Blue Ridge Mountains looming on the horizon. The Hestons were quite a smash. They staged modern plays such as James Thurber's *The Male Animal* and Tennessee Williams's *The Glass Menagerie*—only the second production of Williams's play (the first, which had opened on Broadway in 1945, was still running in New York). By the time their contract was up, the Asheville Theater Board realized that with the Hestons they had lucked into something special. They offered the couple a year's contract at a better salary and more on the horizon.

It would have been a wonderful life, building our own theater, a home and a family in the lovely town of Asheville. But somehow it wasn't what Lydia and I wanted. We talked it through, and decided it was time to go back to and give Broadway one more try.

This time, they struck gold.

WHEN GUTHRIE MCCLINTIC *announced that his wife, Katharine Cornell, would appear in a new production of Shakespeare's* Antony and Cleopatra, *it was big news.*

Every actor's dream: making it in New York City, 1946. This is the first "penthouse" we were ever in . . . let alone *lived* in.

Katharine Cornell was born in 1898 in Berlin. In 1921 she married Guthrie McClintic, and he became her producer and her favorite director. Before long, Cornell-McClintic was a byword in the annals of the American theater. When Heston returned to New York with Lydia in August 1947, he decided to audition for the Shakespeare production.

Not surprisingly, the hall outside the Radio City offices of Cornell-McClintic was already crowded. Inside, the waiting room was packed. There were a dozen or so actors sitting smugly behind a three-foot railing, which I figured was the space reserved for actors with appointments. I didn't have an appointment, but I do have long legs. When the secretary stepped away to lead one actor to the inner office, I quickly swung over the railing and sank into the chair just vacated. It was a small step, but quite possibly the one that made all the difference.

The day wore on until I was the only applicant left. The secretary sized me up with obvious suspicion.

"And who are you? I have no other name on the list."

"What?! That can't be! Maynard Morris made the appointment," I said, treading water now, since I'd never met the distinguished MCA agent, let alone set foot inside the MCA offices. The secretary frowned.

"All right then," she sighed. "Mr. McClintic has a little time. Follow me." I followed her, heart pounding."

A few seconds later, McClintic, the legendary mentor of America's greatest actors, was staring down his desk at a tall, innocent-

Above: The beautiful Katharine Cornell.
Right: A scene from Cornell-McClintic's Broadway production of *Antony and Cleopatra*.

looking youth. McClintic noticed Heston's height, since his wife liked tall men around her onstage. Besides, it was getting late. He took pity on the poor young sod, who had probably spent half the day camping out in his front office, and decided to give him a break. He reached for a copy of the play.

"So, Mr. Heston," he said, "care to try a cold reading?"

I took the book. It was open to the last page, at Caesar's elegy mourning the death of the two lovers. I cleared my throat, and began:

> *High events as these*
> *Strike those that make them; and their story is*
> *No less in pity than his glory which*
> *Brought them to be lamented . . .*

The elegy finished; I returned the book. It was quiet. Off in the corner of the office somewhere, an old clock ticked the seconds away. McClintic was looking at me with a strange expression on his face. Then he made up his mind.

"Not bad. Come back tomorrow at ten."

A few weeks later, Heston made his professional Broadway debut. He was cast as Proculeius, Caesar's aide-de-camp, who is sent to fetch Cleopatra after her lover Antony has been killed.

Everyone agreed that Katharine Cornell positively *glowed* in the part of Cleopatra—the last major role of her long and distinguished career. The critics also had kind words to say about the rest of the cast, which included, among others, Eli Wallach and Maureen Stapleton. Most importantly, the play was a hit—rare on Broadway, and rarer still for a Shakespeare play. For Heston, it was like having died and gone to heaven, which is what he was more or less expected to do each night. In Act 5, scene 2, McClintic had told him to leap off a large tomb and forcefully seize Cleopatra, who was hiding within.

> CLEOPATRA
> *(Drawing a dagger)*
> Quick, quick, good hands.
>
> PROCULEIUS
> Hold, worthy lady, hold:
> Do not yourself such wrong, who are in this
> Relieved, but not betray'd.

One evening near the end of the play's New York run, Heston checked in early. The stage manager spotted him and gave him an angry scowl.

"Heston! Miss Cornell wants to see you in her dressing room. Now!"

So off I went to Miss Cornell's abode, a thousand thoughts spinning in my head. I've screwed up. I've done something very wrong. But what? No matter, I'm going to get fired. But why? Miss Cornell wouldn't fire me, McClintic would. Suddenly, I stopped dead in my tracks. There could only be one explanation. She wants my body. I broke out in sweat. Oh My God, she wants to go to bed with me.

I knock on the door. Miss Cornell's maid opens up and casts a disapproving look. She says, "Go on inside." I did. And there she is, the diva of Broadway, the reigning queen of American theater, all beauty and glamour—and dressed in nothing but a thin, silky robe. She beckons me closer.

"Come in. I want to show you something." As in slow-motion, I step forward. Katharine Cornell's hand slips down to the hem of her robe, and lifts it. I swallow hard and look down on a bare thigh, long, slim, and luscious. With a large bruise on it. "When you throw me across your leg to take my dagger away, " she says, "I always land on your sword. Do you suppose you could wear it on your other hip, just for that scene?"

Relieved and dismayed at the same time, I stammer my apologies and assure her that I will wear my sword on the other side—in fact, I will not wear it at all, I will get rid of the damned thing, I will, I shall . . .

But by then Miss Cornell had, slowly and gently, worked young Mr. Heston out of her dressing room, the hint of a smile on her lips.

Meanwhile, Lydia had made a giant leap forward. She had a real agent, Maynard Morris of MCA no less. She went on to play Lady Anne in *Richard III* off-Broadway. Of course, Lydia asked Maynard to work his magic for her husband as well. He did. He got him a part—as an understudy. The play, *Leaf and Bough*, was directed by Rouben Mamoulian, noted for his many successful Hollywood films and his staging of *Oklahoma!* in 1943. Before their Broadway opening, the cast of *Leaf and Bough* left for Boston for a try-out run. Here, as luck would have it, Heston got to play the part for real. After a second try-out run in Philadelphia, they opened on Broadway—and lasted for about a week. "Should have been called *Bow and Leave*," one witty critic mused.

Once again, Heston was out of work. He sighed, and looked from their tiny flat in Hell's Kitchen at the skyline of New York. Little did he know that that horizon was changing.

IT WAS CALLED TELEVISION. Before 1947, it didn't amount to much. The television industry at that time was mostly centered in and around New York, which had the country's largest concentration of installed television sets. Programs, such as there were, went on the air "live" in the era before videotape. Advertisers were skeptical, for television offered an audience that was hardly worth the trouble. Even so, NBC was the front runner in the "ratings."

Then, in 1947, the World Series was played between the New York Yankees and the Brooklyn Dodgers. Since the Series was going to be an all-New York affair, some bright young executive at NBC suggested that NBC should air the games on television, as something of a stunt. NBC management liked the idea and aired the games. The show was a blockbuster. Almost overnight, the World Series catapulted television from relative obscurity to the nation's fastest-growing entertainment medium. People lined up to buy TV sets. Between 1947 and 1956, Americans owning sets zoomed from 2 percent to 70 percent of all households.

With NBC's sudden surge forward, CBS realized that it could no longer hold off; it had to develop its own television network or be left behind. Now that they had found an audience, the problem facing the networks was how to *hold on* to their viewers. It was not sufficient to air a popular program once in a while; it had to be developed into a series that could build audience loyalty, just as radio had done. And so the television series was born.

NBC dipped into its pool of radio stars and rolled out one smash-hit series after another: Milton Berle's "Texaco Star Theater," Ed Sullivan's "Toast of the Town," and many others. Variety shows ruled supreme, for the simple reason that people thought of television as radio with moving pictures. Berle's and Sullivan's variety shows gave them movement in spades, with lots of frolicking, jumping, and other visual slapstick.

CBS, too, dipped into its repertory and chose a relatively new radio drama called "Studio One" to convert into a TV series. Drama was prestigious and could hold on to an audience, and television needed all the prestige it could get. Hollywood considered television a major threat to its theatrical business. Studios forbade their actors to work for television and hoped that if they starved television of its premium talent it would simply go away. Broadway wasn't very sympathetic, either: *Most Broadway actors considered television sort of tacky. Serious actors didn't do that kind of thing; nor directors, God knows.* In addition to which, it hardly paid enough for an actor to go through the trouble of performing a play just once, and "live" at that.

CBS commissioned one of its veteran producers, Worthington Miner, to produce "Studio One." Miner decided to stage an honest-to-goodness Shakespeare play in order to show Broadway and Hollywood that television could do Shakespeare just as well as anyone. He summoned one of his assistant producers and told him to go scouting for actors on Broadway. "Find me actors who have done Shakespeare before," he said. "I don't care if they're big or not. Just make sure they can do Shakespeare, and drag 'em in here."

Live television was the big break. Of course, television was probably the most significant development in the moving image since sound was added to the movies. It had the same kind of impact. I wasn't very smart, but I did realize that something very important was about to happen.

The first play for "Studio One" was Julius Caesar, *with Robert Keith as Brutus. Somewhat to my disappointment, I got cast as Cinna, a minor role. I was secretly hoping my Cornell-McClintic credit would get me a more respectable part. But, as luck would have it, Keith was sick one day during rehearsals. I filled in for him during the readings. When we quit, Frank Schaffner, the director, took me aside. "Could you stick around for a minute?" he asked, and off he went to get Tony Miner.*

When they came back, Tony said, "Frank here wants me to hear you read something."

"Okay," I said. "Sure. What do you want me to read?"

"How about Antony's funeral oration. Are you familiar with that?"

Was he kidding? I had won my scholarship to Northwestern with that speech. It is the showiest, shortest, and easiest of the parts. I mean, if you can't make an impression with that speech, you have no business doing Shakespeare. So they listened, nodded a bit, and thanked me. That was that. The next day, I went back to my role as Cinna.

One beautiful Sunday evening in the spring of 1949, between 7:30 p.m. and 8:30 p.m., history was made: Julius Caesar *went on the air for the first time, and so did Heston.*

Miner and Schaffner did not forget Heston's impromptu performance as Antony. He got the lead in the next play "Studio One" was about to stage: Jane Eyre, *opposite Mary Sinclair. That was followed by* Of Human Bondage, Wuthering Heights *(again with Mary Sinclair), and* The Taming of the Shrew *(with Phyllis Kirk).*

I did Chekhov, Shaw, and Turgenev. You see, nobody really knew what television was supposed to be like. Of course, the networks who owned the technology didn't have a clue as to how to program it, because they had never done that kind of thing before. So more or less by default, this new entertainment medium was left in the hands of a bunch of unemployed 24-year-olds—including, fortunately, me.

And I wasn't the only one. A whole generation of future Hollywood actors got their first taste of acting in front of the cameras of CBS's "Studio One": Anne Bancroft, Jack Lemmon, Yul Brynner, James Dean, John Forsythe, Walter Matthau, and Leslie Nielsen. There were directors like George Hill, Sidney Lumet, Johnny Frankenheimer, and Frank Schaffner. Authors like Rod Serling, Paul Monash, and Paddy Chayefsky wrote the teleplays.

For us as actors, the key advantage was that we were learning a new technology and establishing an audience identity before we ever made movies. We were already known by the time we got to Hollywood. And that applied to the actors as well as the directors and writers. In short, we got to invent *television.*

Lydia's acting career was taking flight as well. She was cast

With Mary Sinclair in the "Studio One" production of *Jane Eyre*, directed by Frank Schaffner.

as the lead in a modern play called *Detective Story* directed by Sidney Kingsley. Their early successes did not go unnoticed: Chuck and Lydia both received *Theatre World* Awards as two of the most promising actors in America.

And then, out of the blue, David Bradley called again from Chicago. "Chuck," he said, "you've gotta get out here. That last thing on TV was terrible, just terrible. You see, I'm going to do Julius Caesar *and I want you to come do it for me."*

"Well David," I said, "that's okay, but I can't do it for free. I'm a professional actor now."

"Mmmmm," David said. "All right. I'll pay you."

I think he paid me fifty dollars a week—which was slightly below the Equity minimum which I'd been working for, but you know, it is such a great part. I simply couldn't pass it up.

The budget for *Julius Caesar* was only $11,000, but Bradley profited from the fact that Chicago is dotted with stately classical buildings that could quite easily pass as temples in the Roman Forum. Thus,

Above: As Mark Antony In David Bradley's *Julius Caesar*, 1950. Right: We recorded the sound for Julius Caesar without guide tracks, which was quite a task.

Above: Our names on the marquee for the first time. Actually, Lydia was better in her part than I was in mine. Right: With Lydia in *Detective Story*, 1957, a play to which we would return many times in the years to come.

Bradley was able to evoke the grandeur of Rome—on the cheap. The 16mm film was not theatrically released, but it did create quite a stir at various film festivals.

Meanwhile, back in New York, Tony Miner was planning his next "Studio One" project.

Miner called me to his office, and Frank Schaffner was already there. So Miner turns to us and says, "Listen guys, could you do a 90-minute version of Macbeth?" We looked at one another and nodded. "Sure, why not," Schaffner said. "Well, could you do it with, ah, ten days rehearsal?" Miner asked. "Sure," I said, not even thinking about it. "I've done that part before."

Frank Schaffner came up with an idea to make the production more interesting—more visual. He decided to give Macbeth sort of an alter ego, a companion, that he would turn to in the course of his soliloquies. Frank rented this huge Irish wolfhound that Macbeth would talk to. It turned out to be a wonderful idea.

Ten days later, exhausted, Heston played *Macbeth*. It was CBS's first nation-wide broadcast, all the way to the West Coast. It even reached as far as a tiny hamlet called Hollywood.

The Lure of

Film is the only art form whose raw materials are so expensive that the artist cannot afford to buy them for himself.

HOLLYWOOD

IN 1944, PRODUCER HAL WALLIS did an unusual thing. At the age of forty-five, he was one of the pre-eminent star-makers of Hollywood, the producer of Warner Brothers films from *Little Caesar* (1930) to *Casablanca* (1942)—a man, in short, who had made Hollywood history many times over. That year, something happened at the Oscar ceremonies that changed his life. His surprise hit *Casablanca*, starring Humphrey Bogart and Ingrid Bergman, won the Academy Award for Best Picture. When it was announced, he got out of his seat, but the head of the studio, Jack Warner, beat him to the punch, hurrying to the stage to accept the Oscar himself. Wallis was furious and did an impetuous thing: He quit, ending a twenty-year association with Warner Brothers.

Wallis moved out of the Warners lot and, as he said later, "set up the first independent motion picture production company since Chaplin, Pickford, and Fairbanks founded United Artists." However, in 1944 the studio system was still in full force. Wallis realized that he needed an alliance with a strong studio that could help him attract major funding and secure distribution at home and abroad. In the end, he settled on Paramount. It turned out to be a prosperous association, but with a difference: Hal was his own man. Within reason, he could do what he liked. He was an independent wheel inside the machine of an old-fashioned Big Studio—and Hal Wallis was going to change the way Hollywood did business.

WALLIS WAS ON THE LOOKOUT for strong, muscular actors. He believed that World War II had left the public craving for heroes with good looks. That's how he had stumbled on Kirk Douglas, "a lithe, barrel-chested six-footer with a mop of wavy hair," who in 1945, after serving in the Navy during the war, appeared in a rather dim Broadway play called *The Wind Is Ninety*. Douglas, a son of Russian immigrants like Wallis himself, had just been decommissioned from the Navy after a crippling accident in his anti-submarine unit. He made his electrifying movie debut in 1946 in *The Strange Love of Martha Ivers*, produced by Hal Wallis Productions and starring Barbara Stanwyck. Two years later, Wallis hired another masculine superstar-in-the-making, Burt Lancaster, and put him under contract for four pictures.

In 1949, Wallis came across another fellow with the "rugged" look. He was reminded of a *New York Times* review that described the tall actor as "a rough-hewn sort of chap who looks like a triple-threat

Above: Hal Wallis, the producer who brought me to Hollywood. Right: William Dieterle, the director of my first Hollywood film, *Dark City*.

halfback on a Midwestern college football team." Wallis believed he had seen the young actor in a telecast of some sort.

"*Macbeth*," says Heston. "He saw me in *Macbeth*."

"Well, he may have also seen you in *Jane Eyre*," Lydia interjects.

"Yes, that's true; I think he saw *Jane Eyre*. And also, I'm told—although I don't know—he may have seen the *Julius Caesar* I did for David too."

Hal did not say. What he did say to Heston, after he called him on the telephone, was to get himself to Hollywood right away.

WALTER SELTZER, Wallis's head of publicity, was waiting for Heston at the airport, carrying a not-very-good 8-by-10 glossy of him. When Heston appeared, Seltzer compared the photo to the original several times before approaching him.

"Are you Charlton Heston?" Seltzer asked.

"That's right."

"Well," Seltzer declared, "if Wallis signed you off this still, he's in for a nice surprise."

Hal Wallis wasn't surprised, but he did something he had never done in his entire life. He signed Heston on the spot. There was no screen test, no checking of references. True, Wallis, the inveterate talent-chaser, was impressed—but he also knew that Warner Brothers was after this young man. For all he knew, they could have already made Chuck an offer —which in fact, they had. Wallis felt good about Heston. The young man exuded an air of quiet professionalism, combined with a certain down-to-earth humility, and an eagerness to learn.

Initially, I said no to Warners, which put me at odds with the major studios. The thing is, I already had a career in television and a modest reputation on the stage. I was interested in doing movies, but not at the expense of giving up the career I'd built back in New York. And there was the rub, you see. Hollywood wouldn't let its actors appear on television—me or anyone else.

I guess Hal Wallis surprised everyone in Hollywood by agreeing to my terms. As an independent, he had the freedom to do so. What's more, Hal knew that the studio system was changing. So he gave me what no one else had gotten up to that point: an independent contract with the right to do plays and television. It horrified the industry. No one, with the possible exception of Marlon Brando, had ever gotten away with an independent contract like that. Hal signed me for five films. In between, I was free to accept roles in other films or do plays on television or the stage.

The Heston contract was a landmark, for it was the first successful attack on the iron grip with which studios had controlled their talent. The studios were not amused. Perhaps the most irate of all was Jack Warner, who'd believed that Chuck was already in *his* bag. The bad blood between Warner and Wallis did not improve the situation any. In frustration, Warner turned his wrath on MCA, who were on record as young Heston's agents, and threw them off the Warners lot. This, in essence, banned most of MCA's other clients from the Warners studios. In the general uproar, the Screen Actors Guild was called in to arbitrate, and the fight continued for quite some time.

It was certainly an auspicious start. Heston hadn't yet appeared on a foot of film, and already he was a cause célèbre in Hollywood.

MY FIRST PICTURE *for Hal Wallis was a* film noir. *As films noir go, it wasn't bad. In fact, it was distinguished by the fact that it had several songs, so I suppose you could call it the only musical* film noir *ever made.*

Many German-born directors seem to have been attracted to the *film noir* genre, which is characterized by a dark psychological atmosphere and shadowy, mood-lit photography portraying a world of corruption, violence, and sexual bargaining. *Dark City* (1950), directed by William Dieterle, was no exception. Dieterle, born in Ludwigshafen, Germany in 1893, had flirted with the German Expressionist style, made famous by Robert Wiene's art film *The Cabinet of Dr. Caligari* in 1919. In Germany in 1923, Dieterle had directed his first film, in which he had cast a demure, twenty-one-year-old actress named Marlene Dietrich, and made several more films there before emigrating to Hollywood in 1930.

Above and right: Lizabeth Scott, who played the nightclub singer in *Dark City*, had a very unique presence on screen. Opposite: This is the first tailored suit I ever owned—courtesy of Hal Wallis. He let me keep it, too (the nose is my own).

In *Dark City*, Heston played Danny Haley, a World War II veteran who has trouble adjusting to peacetime life while trying to figure out if he is in love. In the meantime, he employs his considerable skill at poker to "shake" a hapless victim, Arthur Winant (played by Don DeFore). Unfortunately, Winant was playing with borrowed money, and after the game he hangs himself in despair. Winant's brother finds out that the game was a setup, and decides to track down the dishonest poker player. For the duration of the film, Haley is on the run, trying to dodge his unseen assassin while flirting with Winant's demure widow, Victoria (Vivica Lindfors), and with the poison-sweet nightclub singer Fran (Lizabeth Scott).

William Dieterle was a very good director. I think he did a very good job with it. I certainly had no problems with him and I hope he had none with me. When the cameras started to roll, I realized how invaluable my television experience had been. You see, film and television have more in common than most people realize. In television, too, you have to hit your marks; you have to match the movements, remember the angles, and watch the shadows. And unlike those actors who came to Hollywood fresh from the stage, I had learned to do all that.

Other than that, I was as green as grass. I had never heard of film noir. It was my first movie, and that was all there was to it. My co-star was Lizabeth Scott, a sultry blonde with black eyebrows and a low, sexy voice. She had an interesting "bond to me, come to me, go from me" quality that served her well, I think. She had a unique presence on screen. And as for me, when in doubt I reverted to my "brooding look," which I thought matched the mood of the movie.

Unfortunately for Dieterle, the press may have had its fill of *film noir* by 1950. "Melodramatic suspense," wrote film critic Bosley Crowther in the *New York Times*. Heston's performance, on the other hand, found much favor. "His film debut is impressive" was the verdict in *Variety*, and "Hal Wallis has got himself another Burt Lancaster" according to the *Los Angeles Times*. Crowther agreed: "Mr. Heston, who has worked for the stage and video (*sic*), has something more than appearance to recommend him for dramatic roles. He has a quiet and assertive magnetism, a youthful dignity and a plainly potential sense of timing that is the good actor's *sine qua non*."

Dark City went on to do respectable business, due in part to the whirlwind tour on which Paramount sent Heston to promote the film. *It was rough. We did fourteen cities in twenty-three days, always staying just ahead of the film's opening. I learned something that is crucial to an actor—how to do interviews. No doubt that was reflected in the good press we got out of it.* Throughout it all, publicist Walter Seltzer never left his side. In due course, the Seltzers and the Hestons became close friends.

Chuck returned to Hollywood to pack his bags, return the keys to the apartment that Paramount had provided for him, and fly back to New York.

But what about the Paramount contract? What about his next film? Where was Hal Wallis? Chuck began to realize that there was a price to pay for his open-ended deal after all.

I guess Hal had already realized that there was no point in building me up as his star, as he had done with Kirk Douglas and Burt Lancaster before. He wasn't going to have any control anyway pretty soon, so in essence he was perfectly willing to do one picture for me, and then sell the other commitments for whatever he could get. This, as it turned out, was quite a lot of money. That was fair, I could understand that. But, mind you, there I was. The beginning of the turnover.

HESTON'S PERFORMANCE in *Dark City* got him noticed. Later that year, he got called to Hollywood by William Wyler. Wyler was *big*. Just four years earlier, he'd won his *second* Oscar for Best Director, for *The Best Years of Our Lives* (his first was for *Mrs. Miniver* in 1942). Wyler was looking around for a new project. As luck would have it, it was a film version of the play *Detective Story*, in which Lydia was still playing the female lead on Broadway.

I was elated to hear that William Wyler wanted to test me for the lead. Dark City was a modest success, but I needed something more substantial to keep the momentum in Hollywood going. I flew to the West Coast to do my screen test, brimming with confidence. I told myself there was no question I'd get the part. Mind you, I always think that about any part. Why I didn't get some, I don't know, but you have to think that you will get it, or you won't get any of them. I thought it was all taken care of, but I was wrong. Willy Wyler had me cool my heels in the Beverly Hills hotel for four days, at Paramount's expense. Then, one day, I heard on Louella Parson's radio show that Willy had cast Kirk Douglas. Just like that. It was a very tough thing to take—a shot right between the eyes.

Looking back at it now, I realize that I was a bit too young and too green for the role. Kirk was then coming into the peak period of his career, and he turned out to be very good in one of Willy Wyler's best films. And, as it turned out, not getting the part was the best thing that could ever have happened to me. In any case, I packed my bags and drove to the Paramount lot to say my good-byes. That done, I got in my car and headed for the gate.

Big events often turn on the smallest decisions. Later, Chuck would think back and wonder, *What if I had left earlier? What if I had hung around a bit longer? What if I had chosen another gate?* But he didn't. He headed toward a gate named for the building next to it, both of which were named for the man who worked in it—the famous producer-director Cecil B. DeMille, who at that moment happened to be standing on the steps of the building.

I had met DeMille—everybody eventually met DeMille, I suppose. Mr. DeMille made it his business to take a brief look at all the new talent that came through Paramount. It was very simple: You were invited to the commissary to sit at his table for lunch. You sat down, had some coffee, talked for ten minutes, and then you got up. I did it, too. So here I was, driving off the lot with the top down on a Packard convertible I had bought from my father, and I saw DeMille standing with some of his people, his entourage, on the steps of his building.

Imagine the moment: The Packard is approaching now, its engine purring, its olive-green a splash of polish against the concrete of the lot. DeMille's head turns. Heston, who has already spotted the great man from afar, wonders what to do. Should he stop to say hello? Should he simply keep going? Should he, at the very least, wave to him?

DeMille, still in conversation, glances at the young man in his convertible. His brow creases while part of his brain goes searching through his mental card file, trying to match that big, smiling face with a name. He sees the blur of a hand, in a friendly wave, though with slight hesitation, deferring the respect that is due. And then the green Packard passes through the gate and is gone.

DeMille pauses. His secretary waits.

"Who was that, just now?" the director asks.

The secretary is already flipping through her notebook. "Charlton Heston. Young Broadway actor. Hal Wallis brought him out. He made one picture, *Dark City*. You ran it last week." The secretary pauses. Sometimes, with just a few words like these, a career can be made or broken. "You didn't like it."

"Mmmmmm," says DeMille, thinking. He is still staring at the gate, but the young Broadway actor is long gone. "Actually, I liked the way he *waved* just now. We'd better get him in."

A few days later, Charlton Heston was cast as a circus manager, the lead role in Cecil B. DeMille's biggest project to date, *The Greatest Show on Earth*.

"THERE ARE TIMES," DEMILLE recalled in 1959, "when it takes me a long time to reach decisions. Sometimes, I hear and heed opportunity's first knock." On that occasion, the knock had taken the form of a small notice in the *Hollywood Reporter* in 1949. The article noted that the circus of Ringling Brothers and Barnum & Bailey, ringmasters to the world, had floated the idea of making a film. Uncharacteristically, DeMille, without considering the idea at length or consulting his trusted circle of consultants and aides, simply walked into the office of Henry Ginsberg, Paramount's head of production, and sold him on the idea. It was an auspicious beginning, for *The Greatest Show on Earth* would be unlike any other film he made.

My very first shot for DeMille. I leaped out of the Jeep, then fell over a ring curb. He didn't fire me. Jimmy Stewart is the clown.

Soon, word began to spread that DeMille was casting the movie. The town's leading actresses tried different methods to attract the director's attention. Among them was Paulette Goddard, Charlie Chaplin's third ex-wife, who had starred in several DeMille films. Goddard sent DeMille a telegram that read:

HOPE ALL THOSE RUMORS ABOUT MY GOING INTO THE GREATEST SHOW ON EARTH ARE TRUE. AM RETURNING MONDAY TO SIGN THE CONTRACT.

UNBEKNOWNST TO Miss Goddard, however, she had fallen out of DeMille's favor when, in the role of a slave girl in *Unconquered* (1947), she got scared of some fireballs. Obviously, such a person was not the best choice to perform circus acts.

Betty Hutton's ploy fared no better at first, even though it was executed with considerably more style. The blond World War II pinup and star of MGM's Technicolor extravaganza *Annie Get Your Gun* (1950) sent DeMille a huge bouquet of flowers topped with a miniature figure of herself dangling on a trapeze. On receiving it,

DeMille asked one of his aides to bring him a photograph of Hutton in a bathing suit, took one look, and spoke his verdict: "Too heavy on the hips." Undaunted, the "Blonde Bombshell" of World War II fame demanded an audience. She was admitted, and DeMille repeated his opinion in her presence: "You are too heavy on the hips."

Hutton solemnly promised to go on a crash diet to produce the nimble limbs the director was looking for. DeMille gave her the female lead and sent her a telegram assuring her, MY HEART BELONGS TO ANNIE, WITH OR WITHOUT A GUN.

Casting the male roles was a bit easier. Jimmy Stewart, who by then had a pick of roles, wanted to play a clown, any clown. Unfortunately, there was no clown in any of the lead roles, so DeMille had one written in. The part became that of a clown, "Buttons," who had been a physician but was accused of committing euthanasia on his wife and so was on the run from the law. DeMille liked it, but ruled that Stewart should never take his clown paint off while playing the part. The only time Stewart's handsome features are seen undisguised is in the form of a small photograph, used by

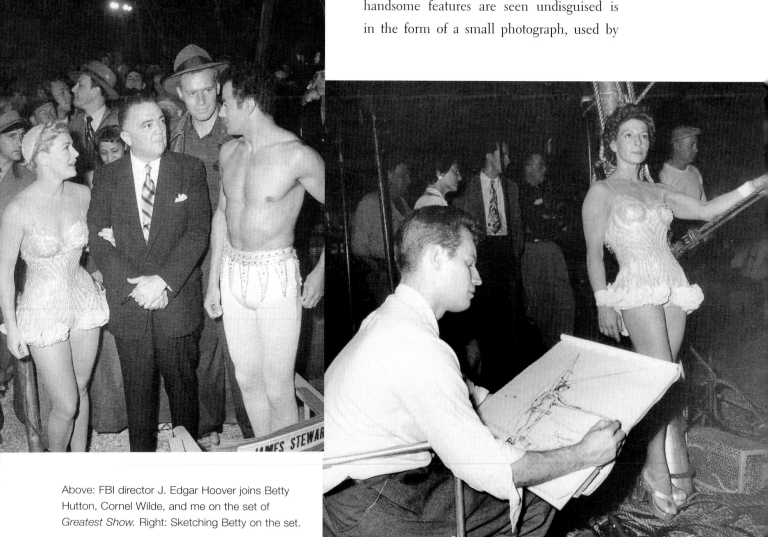

Above: FBI director J. Edgar Hoover joins Betty Hutton, Cornel Wilde, and me on the set of *Greatest Show*. Right: Sketching Betty on the set.

CHARLTON HESTON'S HOLLYWOOD

detectives to track him down. True to form, Stewart designed his own makeup, as real clowns do.

The story of *The Greatest Show on Earth* is relatively simple: The circus manager, Brad Braden, a man with sawdust in his blood (played by Heston) is too preoccupied with all the details of running the circus to notice anything else, including the loving attentions of a trapeze girl, Holly (Hutton). Holly will do anything to capture Brad's attention, including a death-defying trapeze stunt that he has forbidden her to attempt. Of course, she does it anyway, and this leads to their first public quarrel, and then some. Soon, "The Great Sebastian," a glamorous aerialist with a vague Hungarian accent (Cornel Wilde) appears and wastes no time luring the pouting Holly into his own well-muscled arms. However, Sebastian is severely injured in a fall, Buttons the clown is tracked down by the law, and the whole circus suffers a nasty train crash that leaves the company in tatters. But, since this is the circus of make-believe, everyone recovers and the show goes on.

It may not have been a story that would grab headlines, but as DeMille reminded himself, the story was never the point of *Greatest Show*. It was the circus.

It was wonderful to spend time with the circus people. And very patient and understanding they were with all of us, which believe me, was quite a task. In fact, many of the cast had to master some amazing skills. Hutton and Wilde had to look like they knew what they were doing as they flew through the air from one bar to the next. Dorothy Lamour was hung by her teeth and spun around in the so-called "iron jaw" act. Lyle Bettger learned how to handle elephants, and was nearly crushed when, in the eyes of one particularly irritable beast, he failed to live up to the task.

Perhaps the most courageous of all was Cornel Wilde, who was horrified to discover that he had a fear of heights. However, Cornel feared the wrath of DeMille more, so he stuck to his act as a daredevil trapeze artist. DeMille was not so easily fooled. One day, when Wilde was trying on some high-heeled clogs, DeMille said, "Better not wear those, Mr. Wilde. Aren't you afraid of heights?"

My own preparation was a lot simpler. I simply had to pick a hat. That sounds easy, but it wasn't, since DeMille felt it was a very important creative decision. One day, he called me into his office, which was covered with at least fifty fedora hats. "It is very important that you wear the right hat," he said. "Shoes I don't care about, but your hat is in every shot, even more so in close-ups." For the next hour or so, I tried on every hat in his office before the right one was found.

When shooting on The Greatest Show *started, I had little else to do but to walk around and bellow orders to my handlers, linesmen, and performers: "Pick that up."*

"Don't handle the animal like that." "Go get the doctor to prescribe something for that elephant," and so forth. But my very first scene almost ended in disaster. It was my first take. I was supposed to drive in, chatting with Jimmy, and then look up to see that Betty Hutton is doing this trapeze act that I told her not to do. I leaped out of the jeep and raced over to grab the ropes and lower her down to safety. Except I tripped on the ring curb, and fell flat in the ring. Imagine—my very first shot for DeMille. "Cut!" DeMille yelled.

Slowly, I got back to my feet, brushing the sawdust off my jacket, not quite daring to look at Mr. DeMille while anticipating the trashing that was sure to follow. But he was most cordial. "I think we'll do another take on that, Chuck," DeMille said. "Maybe, if you could get over the ring curb this time, it would be better."

As I got into the jeep and drove back to the starting position, Jimmy Stewart cast a sideward glance. "Waaall, Chuck, " he drawled, "it'll only get better from here."

The second challenge I faced was a bit more hazardous. The scene takes place immediately after the train crash. As the smoke clears, my character is pinned down by the wreckage of a cage, unable to move. I guess Mr. DeMille figured

Opposite: I never wore boots and britches in *Greatest Show*. They must have dressed me up as an elephant trainer for some P. R. stills. The elephant did fine. Left: With James Stewart, Betty Hutton, Gloria Grahame, Cornel Wilde, and a couple of extras, after the train crash. Above: DeMille's sound man.

Left: Dancing badly with my girl, who dances wonderfully, November 28, 1952. Above: With Betty and Mr. DeMille at the opening of *Greatest Show*.

I might lose my nerve. . . . The steel bars of the cage pinned me down very effectively. The plan was to have a black panther leap out of the cage and escape through the bent bars. Of course, I was in no position to argue about this because there I was, pinned down to the hilt. So they got the panther, but the animal stayed in the back of the cage, and was disinclined to go anywhere else.

"Don't worry, I'll just goose him in the ass with an air hose," said the trainer.

"Don't goose him in the ass with an air hose," I hissed between my teeth.

So they did.

The panther, seething with rage, jumped right on top of my chest, adding to my already considerable discomfort. I decided it was best to play dead, but let me tell you, panthers have horribly bad breath.

Lydia was on the scene throughout the filming, gripping a still camera that DeMille's stillsman had taught her how to use. "I was watching all of this," Lydia says, "and I was quite terrified."

"*You* were terrified?" Chuck laughs. "*I* was terrified!"

"Well," Lydia says, "finally they brought the elephant who was supposed to lift the cage that was pinning him down."

"Ninya was her name. A very good elephant."

"But there was a nail on the ground and it went right through the elephant's foot. She trumpeted and pounded her feet and—"

"There I was . . . dead again!" He laughs.

"So they soothed the elephant," Lydia continues, "and then she quite readily lifted the cage off, and Chuck was free. I must confess, I was terrified." Through all of this, perhaps because she was so frightened, Lydia gripped the camera tightly and never let go of it. Ever since, she has accompanied Heston to all the sets as his private still photographer, shooting an invaluable visual history of his career.

MUCH TO PARAMOUNT'S relief, *Greatest Show* was as much a hit with the critics as it was with the public. "Everything in this lusty triumph of circus showmanship and movie skill betokens the way with the spectacular of the veteran Mr. DeMille," gushed the *New York Times*. "Here, against the background of a circus, all the faults that caused such critical mutterings about [DeMille's] *Samson and Delilah* are converted into positive virtues," was the opinion in *Saturday Review*. *Variety* found the film attractive to the "sophisticates as well as the hordes who've traditionally so well patronized DeMille's epics." "DeMille and the circus are fated to each other," agreed *Time*.

However, most critics also agreed that the story was too synthetic, too trite, and too obvious an extraneous element in this great spectacle about the "real" circus— although Bosley Crowther in the *Times* concluded that "the rambling criss-cross of complications in these circus people's lives" probably reflected the real goings-on in life under the big top.

On January 10, 1952, *The Greatest Show on Earth* opened big and went on to become a smashing box-office success. In its first year it earned $12 million, setting a record for 1952 and beating another great epic, *Quo Vadis*, which brought in $10.5 million.

The picture was also a personal triumph for DeMille. At long last, at the Academy Awards ceremony on March 13, 1953—the first time the Oscars were broadcast on television—he was awarded the coveted Irving Thalberg Award, and *The Greatest Show on Earth* won the Oscar for Best Picture in the drama category. In addition, Fredric M. Frank and his fellow screenwriters took bittersweet revenge on their critics by winning the Academy Award for Best Original Story .

For Heston, the film was the launching platform that he had sought. As he remarked years later, "If you can't make a career out of a DeMille film, I guess you'll never make it in this business."

CHUCK DID MAKE IT. Over the next three years, he starred in eleven films. Obviously, it was not going to be a problem for him to find employment in Hollywood. But the quality of the picture was another matter.

Things started out most promisingly with an independently produced film called *Ruby Gentry*, directed by King Vidor, a silent-era legend on a par with DeMille. *Ruby Gentry* relates the story of an impoverished Southern aristocrat with the improbable name of Boake Tackman (played by Heston), who believes that "a man and his work are one and the same." He is passionately pursued by Ruby (Jennifer Jones), a poor but beautiful young girl who, in the words of the *New York Times*, "generates voltage in tight-fitting jeans." Unfortunately, Tackman cannot reciprocate her love because, for financial reasons, he must marry the daughter of the only banker in town. Her love thus scorned, Ruby marries a gentler soul named Jim Gentry (Karl Malden), but their marriage is not destined to last. After Jim's untimely death, Ruby takes revenge and, unwittingly, causes the death of the man she loves. *This was the first time (though Lord knows it was not the last) that I was killed in a film. It's now eleven deaths, and counting.*

Ruby *was a pretty steamy story for its time, even though, in time-honored Hollywood tradition, the sex was implied, rather than acted out on camera. There is one exception, when we did get pretty physical. King Vidor asked Jennifer to slap me on the cheek. She did. It was no good. "A bit harder, please," Vidor instructed. "It's okay," I said, "just let go. I'll live." Jennifer took a deep breath, swung her arm back, and dealt me this terrific blow to the jaw. For a*

Above: With Jennifer Jones in *Ruby Gentry*. Right: *Ruby Gentry* at the Mayfair and *The Savage* at the RKO Palace, playing side by side.

Left: As William Clark in *Far Horizons*, 1955.
Above: As Ed Bannon in *Arrowhead*, 1953.

moment, I had difficulty staying on my feet. That hurt! I thought. Though not as much as Jennifer's hand. She had broken it.

Ruby Gentry opened in December 1952 to respectable reviews. Heston's screen presence was described as "convincingly muscular." "A bold, adult drama of love and lust," announced *Variety*. Perhaps not surprisingly, the film was a hit. As Vidor proudly recalled in his memoirs, the film also spawned a hit song, "Ruby," which he claimed had been recorded "by at least twenty singers and orchestras."

From late 1952 through 1955, Heston appeared in ten films. Under the terms of the contract with Hal Wallis, he starred in three Westerns (*The Savage, Pony Express,* and *Arrowhead*), three adventures (*The Naked Jungle, The Secret of the Incas,* and *The Far Horizons*), and a period piece (*Lucy Gallant*). In between, he appeared in a film about Andrew Jackson and his wife, Rachel, for 20th Century–Fox, *The President's Lady;* a Columbia Pictures production directed by Irving Rapper, *Bad for Each Other;* and a better-known Universal release, *The Private War of Major Benson.*

The Naked Jungle, based on a short story by Carl Stephenson entitled "Leiningen Versus the Ants," is still shown in reruns on cable television. In it, Heston plays a South American planter who is too involved with growing his cocoa beans to pay much attention to his mail-order bride (played by Eleanor Parker).

In one memorable scene the planter is under attack by a migration of large ants known by the fearsome name of Maribunta. *I'm supposed to pour oil on myself to keep*

A lobby card from *The Private War of Major Benson*, 1955, a rare comedy outing for me.

the ants away because I've got to go blow up the dam. The wardrobe guy had a fit, shouting "No, no, don't use oil; Christ, it'll ruin the wardrobe!"

"Well, for god's sake, what can we do?" I said.

"Syrup, he says, "we'll get syrup."

So they got a five-gallon can of syrup and poured it over me, and right away I drew not only ants, but flies, mosquitoes, and all kinds of nasty things. It was one of the most miserable mornings of my life. You sort of stand around with your hands held far away from your body.

"Today, they would do it with digital effects," says Lydia.

"Yes they would," Chuck admits, "but it wouldn't be half as much fun."

The picture Heston remembers most fondly from this period is his first historical film, *The President's Lady*. In it, he plays Andrew "Old Hickory" Jackson (1767–1845), the seventh president of the United States, and the first president to have been born west of the Appalachians.

I've played thirteen historical figures, three of them more than once, all either saints or presidents, geniuses or generals.

Above: Playing Warbonnet in *The Savage*, 1952. Right: *The Naked Jungle*, 1954, one of the best of my early films.

Other actors have captured the audience's imagination for playing contemporary characters, which I've done ever so rarely. Why is this? What does it say about me, or about those other guys? I'm not sure, but I have an idea. In some cases, it's been because I actually resembled the men I've played—or at the very least look like you'd think this person might have looked. I also got a lot of practice playing historical figures; now, people associate me indelibly with these roles.

As for Jackson, I've played him twice, and still I don't think I've reached all there is of the man. The President's Lady was not written as a comprehensive biography of Jackson, but as a portrait of his lifelong love affair with his wife, Rachel, based on the best-selling novel by Irving Stone. She died just before he became president, when he was also occupied fighting the British and the Creeks and even the United States Bank—all enemies of the Republic, of course. He was the barnstorming commander of the Tennessee militia who cleared the road to Florida from marauding Indians—and who in 1815 had routed a no-less-hostile lot, the British Army at the gates of New Orleans.

Fortunately, we had an actress in the role of Rachel who could keep your interest in the domestic affairs of the Jackson household—Susan Hayward. She made her character a women of flesh and blood—a true frontier girl, a passionate wife, and a devoted companion.

As would become my habit when portraying historical figures, I read as much as there was to read about Jackson, which wasn't much. I did find out that he was six foot three, exactly my height, which was unheard of in his time. I read he was rather touchy about his height, and we used this in a couple of scenes where he knocks his head on

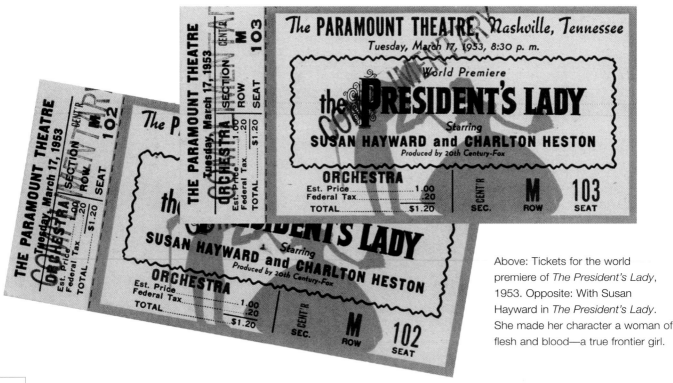

Above: Tickets for the world premiere of *The President's Lady*, 1953. Opposite: With Susan Hayward in *The President's Lady*. She made her character a woman of flesh and blood—a true frontier girl.

Left: With Susan Hayward as Andrew Jackson's wife in *The President's Lady*. She was wonderful in a difficult part. I was lucky to work with her.
Above: Mr. DeMille let me borrow his antique wax statuette of Andrew Jackson.

the low Colonial door lintels. There was also the problem of his accent. At North-western, they'd taught us that the Carolina Smokies still spoke a dialect closest to Elizabethan English. But Old Hickory's parents were Irish, so go figure. In the end, I opted for a modern Carolina accent, for fear that our audience would otherwise be very confused.

When DeMille heard that I was running around town digging up everything I could find about Andrew Jackson, he remembered a twelve-inch statuette which he kept in his office. It had been made as a character study for his first version of The Buccaneer, *in 1938, which also featured Jackson. He let me borrow it, and I kept it for the duration of the shoot. It was a sort of token Jackson, to remind me.*

IN HINDSIGHT, although Heston enjoyed working in some of these pictures, he has second thoughts about his career during those early years.

Perhaps I should have made fewer films in this period. I was in great demand, often filming pictures back to back. A series of leading roles with top billing is fine. But quantity does not always create quality. The directors and screenwriters, while capable, were not the crème de la crème; *neither was the scope of the stories, nor the budgets to back them up.*

Meanwhile, the ever growing specter of an America glued in front of the television set at home rather than spellbound in the theaters was looming larger by the day. Hollywood had to change the way it was doing business. It could no longer ignore television, or forbid its actors from appearing in it. Television, no matter how much they hoped and prayed, was not going to go away. It had to do something to gain an edge in the competition with the upstart medium.

The first action in this campaign was taken on June 10, 1952. On that day, Darryl Zanuck announced that 20th Century–Fox would abandon all B-movie productions, concentrating instead on top-quality, top-budget films. Jack Warner of Warner Brothers, not to be outdone, quickly followed suit. And so the volume of films produced began to shrink. In 1953, Hollywood still had enough productions in the pipeline to release 534 films; but in 1954, only 427 films made it to the theaters, and in 1955, the number had dropped to 392.

The first indications of the strategy's results were encouraging. One studio had spent a considerable portion of its 1953 budget on the lavish costume epic *The Robe*, directed by Henry Koster. It featured the hero of *Samson and Delilah*, Victor Mature, and a young Welsh actor by the name of Richard Burton. But perhaps the most compelling feature of the film was that it was projected on a screen nearly twice as wide as the average film screen. This wide-screen process was based on an optical device known as an anamorphic lens. The principle was simple: you optically compress the image while you shoot, and then spread it out during projection. The patent to this technology was bought by 20th Century–Fox, who called it Cinema-Scope. CinemaScope had its motion-picture debut when *The Robe* opened at the Roxy Theater in New York City on September 16, 1953, and it was a revelation. Crowds lined up around the block to see this marvel, making *The Robe* the top-grossing picture of the year.

All of this was duly noted by Hollywood. By the end of 1953, all the other major studios were busy working on wide-screen films, with each studio using its own version of CinemaScope featuring just enough subtle modifications so as to avoid patent infringement. These included Todd-AO, Metroscope, Panavision, and VistaVision. VisaVision was Paramount's process, and the studio was actively soliciting proposals from its army of producers for a project that would use it to best advantage. This was odd, for it should have been patently obvious to everyone that only one man could do VistaVision justice; only one man could fill it with the grand sweep of extras, color, and costume that the new wide screen demanded. And, as it happened, Cecil B. DeMille had just come up with an idea.

The Ten COM

If you can't make a

career out of two DeMille

films, you shouldn't

be in this business.

MANDMENTS

IN 1953, CECIL B. DEMILLE WAS

IN 1953, CECIL B. DEMILLE WAS seventy-two years old. He could look back at an eminently successful career as a film director—indeed, as the first director ever to be well known to the movie-going public. His name was synonymous with lavish epics populated by casts of thousands. He had made his fortune many times over, and his work had become the stuff of legend before most of his current actors and actresses had even been born. He had Constance DeMille, his wife of fifty-one years, and a large family to retire to. Perhaps it was time to enjoy the sunset years of his life. Most men would have. But DeMille decided to embark on the biggest undertaking ever—a remake of his 1923 epic, *The Ten Commandments*.

"The contract was settled the way Frank Freeman and I always make contracts," DeMille recalled in his 1959 autobiography, with "a few penciled notes on a small piece of paper, and a handshake." At the time, DeMille estimated that the project was going to cost $8 million, an enormous sum in 1953, and even *that* figure, he warned, could not be fully guaranteed. He was right. The final production cost rose to an astounding $13,282,710—the most expensive motion picture ever made up to then. But, as he wrote later, "not once was any question raised about the budget. For the first time in my life, I had a completely free hand."

In terms of casting the movie, DeMille wrote, "I was never in any doubt about who should play the part of Moses."

DeMille was generous in saying that he never had any doubt, but I'm not sure that's entirely true. He must have thought about other possibilities, because he was so meticulous in all his preparations. Since I'd done The Greatest Show on Earth *for him, which won the Academy Award, it was perhaps not a great leap of faith. But mind you, I was a little young for the part.*

DeMille didn't think so. "My choice was strikingly confirmed," he wrote, "when I had a sketch made of Charlton Heston in a white beard and happened to set it beside a photograph of Michelangelo's famous statue of Moses. The resemblance was amazing; and it was not merely an external likeness."

Be that as it may, when Chuck showed up for a first interview with DeMille, it was far from obvious that the Master had made his mind up.

The thing is, DeMille would never actually say that he was considering you for the part. He would simply let it be known to your agent that he would like to talk to you. And so you went. His office would be crowded with books, models, sketches, and even paintings related to the project he was preparing. He sat you down, and then started talking about the film, but from the viewpoint of the character he had in mind for you. It was all very subtle, very understated.

Mr. DeMille didn't tell me he was considering me for Moses. He just did his usual thing, chatting

Above: Yul Brynner as Pharaoh mourns the loss of his son after the final plague. Right: With Anne Baxter as Nefretiri. Opposite: My girl, with Fraser on the way, saying goodbye to Mr. DeMille as we leave for Egypt in September 1954.

about the movie, showing the odd sketch or model, and that was that. Days, weeks would go by and nothing happened. I thought, Perhaps I've blown it. Then, two weeks after the meeting, DeMille asked to see me again. This time, I had learned my lesson. I read up on the time of Ramses II, the Books of Moses in the Bible, and anything else I could get my hands on. When DeMille received me and started to talk, I was ready with some remarks about Moses of my own.

At long last, Paramount made the announcement. DeMille had chosen Heston to play the lead in his most ambitious film.

THE CASTING OF RAMSES II occurred when DeMille was on a family visit in New York and attended a performance of the Broadway hit *The King and I*. When the curtain fell on the first act, he went backstage to meet Yul Brynner, who played the lead role of the King of Siam, and offered him the part of Ramses. Brynner accepted.

The search continued for an actress to play Nefretiri, the wife of Sethi I, until DeMille finally chose Anne Baxter. "The critics were less than kind to my selection," he wrote carefully. The lead cast was rounded out with noted stars Edward G. Robinson (as Dathan), Yvonne De Carlo (as Moses' wife Sephora), and Vincent Price (as Baka). Other roles were played by Henry Wilcoxon, John Carradine, John Derek, Debra Paget, and Judith Anderson: *I was the greenest of them all, but I had the best part.*

In one important aspect, the production was significantly different from the earlier one. The original *Ten Commandments* had been shot on the lot in Los Angeles, whereas this time key scenes would be shot on the very locations where the events, according to tradition, are thought to have taken place. DeMille decided to re-create the city of Per-Rameses close to Giza, the location of the famous pyramids, and to film the epiphany of Moses on the mountain on the actual spot on Mount Sinai in the heart of the Sinai desert.

Preproduction on the film was well under way even before the casting was complete, and after Heston was announced for the role of Moses, he had to submit to endless costume fittings and makeup design sessions.

My personal preproduction was extensive. I had to undergo fittings for some fifteen or twenty costumes, from the intricate platelet armor I wore in my first scene as an Egyptian prince through the burlap rag of the brick pits and the Levite mantle of the Exodus. I have to confess, of the many things I do preparing for a part, I hate fitting wardrobe. It comes right before sitting for studio portraits. Of course, actresses love to do both. That's women for you.

The Moses costumes were designed by an artist of biblical scenes named

My wardrobe included fifteen to twenty different costumes, from the garb of an Egyptian prince (above and center) to the Levite mantle of the Exodus (right).

Arnold Friberg, who had no experience in costume and makeup design. "Everybody thought of Moses as an old, white-haired man," Friberg recalled. "He wasn't. He was a young man, and later a vigorous middle-aged prophet out there in the wilderness with a price on his head—a vigorous leader, a man of God. So I painted pictures of what Heston would look like at various times. Then, one day, Heston had a final fitting with makeup and finished costume. He walked in, and he was no longer the man I knew; he *was* Moses. I had this strange feeling: where have I seen this man before? I realized he was on my drawing board. It was the strangest thing to see the character that you've created come walking in. It was unnerving."

Things were a bit unnerving for Lydia as well. "I wanted very much to go with him to Egypt," she recalls. "I always accompanied Chuck on his travels on location, if it didn't conflict with my own stage work. The only problem was, I was expecting our first child. My obstetrician said, 'If you want this baby, you're not going to go hiking across the Egyptian desert.' I had no choice. I stayed."

Opposite, top: En route via camel to the summit of Mount Sinai, led by Mr. DeMille. St. Catherine's Monastery is in the background. Bottom: Meeting with Egyptian officers in the base camp. No one could foresee that only a year later, tanks would roll over these grounds in the opening days of the Suez Crisis. Above: Mr. DeMille directing from his seat perched high on a Chapman crane in front of the massive gates of Per-Rameses.

JUST BEFORE PRINCIPAL PHOTOGRAPHY was scheduled to begin, a real-world crisis arose when Egypt's King Farouk was deposed in an army coup. DeMille had counted on the use of seven thousand Egyptian troops on horseback to serve as Pharaoh's cavalry as well as thousands of Egyptian builders, artists, and extras to reconstruct the city of Per-Rameses. Farouk's lieutenants had negotiated the deal directly with the Egyptian government, rather than going through U.S. State Department channels. The new leader, it soon transpired, was General Mohammed Naguib. DeMille immediately cabled Naguib to inquire whether the deal was still going to be honored. Luckily, Naguib stood by the contract, and the production went ahead.

The first scene on the schedule was when Moses returns from the mountain on which he has received the tablets with the Ten Commandments.

We set off for the Sinai, in a couple of surplus Land Rovers that had probably served the British before they pulled out of Egypt. We drove across the Suez Canal and headed straight for the Wilderness of Sin. We camped for the night on the shore of the Red Sea, where DeMille and I swam in the milk-warm water. With the glow of the setting sun, it actually looked red.

By the evening of the next day, we reached St. Catherine's Monastery at the foot of Mount Sinai. I stood on the precipice of the monastery walls, built 1,400 years earlier by the Roman Emperor Justinian, and tried to sum up all I had learned about Moses.

I had tried to read everything, from the Old Testament to Freud's book on Moses, and still he escaped me. So many centuries, so many dogmas and scholarly polemics. Who was this man?

DeMille was fascinated with historical detail. He decided on filming as close to the actual summit of Mount Sinai as possible. A special party was organized to make the climb to the top. It takes a grown man in good shape about two hours to walk to the top, but most of the crew opted for camels instead. I declined—I wanted to go the way Moses went, and so I walked. The last half mile was a steep path that culminates in a treacherous stretch of winding steps, and everyone had to walk. The film equipment, which had been carried up by a train of camels and mules, now had to be carried by the Arab crews.

The next day, we filmed the scene in which Moses strides down the mountain after his encounter with the Burning Bush, his face shining with the glory of the divine encounter, his hair and beard transformed. I suddenly had an idea, and I turned to DeMille and said, "I think I should go barefoot in this scene." DeMille just listened. I continued, "Moses has just heard God command him to take off his shoes on that holy ground, then go down and free the Jews from bondage. He's excited, bewildered. The last thing he would have remembered is to put his shoes back on." DeMille stared at me for what felt like an eternity. "All right," he said at last. " I think you're right. We'll do it."

Looking back, DeMille would consider this scene Chuck's finest hour. "He had brought to the role a rapidly maturing skill as an actor and an earnest understanding of the human and spiritual quality of Moses," he wrote later. It was "one of the most moving scenes in the film . . . Moses walking barefoot down the mountainside, his face lifted and filled with the glory and awe of a man who has been face to face with God."

The Arab extras were so impressed that, to them, Heston *was* Moses. As Chuck passed them in costume, they would turn to each other and whisper, "Moussa, Moussa!" As for Heston himself, he remembers the experience vividly: *I wouldn't claim to have found God on that mountain, but I do believe I found Moses.*

AT LAST, THE MASSIVE STRUCTURES of the city of Per-Rameses were complete. The engineers also built a wide avenue, bordered by sixteen sculptured sphinxes, inspired by the approach to the Luxor Temple. There followed the eight thousand costumed extras, plus five thousand cows, asses, sheep, goats, and geese.

DeMille directed from his seat perched high on a Chapman crane. Cinematographer Loyal Griggs supervised a team of cameramen and crew operating four huge VistaVision cameras. Using a powerful P.A. device, DeMille called "Action!" and the

Opposite: This was one of the rare times that the spectacle is so great that you don't have to act. I took a few moments to myself, I turned, stepped to my mark, DeMille called "Action," and the scene began. I never looked back. I just *felt* this mass of humanity following me.

huge tide of men, women, children, and animals was set in motion. The caravan stretched on for four miles, all covered in one vast shot.

"We engaged twenty assistant directors who spoke both Arabic and English," DeMille recalled. "We briefed them each day on the next day's work, and sent them, in costume, into the midst of the Exodus, each one responsible for directing a certain segment of the great moving mass of people, animals, and wagons."

For Heston, it was a defining moment, to be at the head of that vast column of humanity, knowing that they will follow him.

The place itself created a reality in which you don't need to act. I took a few moments to myself, then walked to my mark and lifted my arms:

> *Hear, O Israel! Remember this day,*
> *when the strong hand of the Lord*
> *bears you out of bondage!*

I planted my staff, and stepped forward. I never looked back. I just felt this huge Biblical host following me. On and on they came, the young and the old, the animals and the wagons. It took ten minutes for the entire multitude to pass the rolling Vista-Vision cameras, each camera consuming a full one-thousand-foot reel without stopping once.

DeMille was pleased. The work proceeded on schedule, and it looked like it was all going to come off splendidly. Then one morning, Henry Wilcoxon, who doubled as associate producer, mentioned that one of the VistaVision cameras seemed to have some mechanical trouble. Not content to let the technicians straighten out the problem, DeMille decided to see if he could fix it himself. As it happened, the camera was mounted on top of the 100-foot-high gates of Per-Rameses.

Undaunted, DeMille stepped on a ladder and rapidly climbed to the top. From there, he looked down upon the vast set he had built, his heart surely filled with pride. It was also suddenly pierced by an unbearable pain. DeMille's face turned ashen; he had to hold on tight or he would have doubled over. Henry Wilcoxon was close behind and, with Henry's help, DeMille made his way back to the ground, where he very nearly collapsed.

Fortunately, his personal physician, Max Jacobson, happened to be on the set. The patient was rushed to his bedroom in the villa in Giza. The best cardiologists in Cairo were summoned. They ordered DeMille to stay in an oxygen tent for two weeks, followed by two months of rest. DeMille listened patiently to what they had to say and thanked them. Once the physicians had left, he let his intentions be known. "Tomorrow is Sunday. I'll rest. Monday, I'll go back to work."

"You're taking a big risk," Dr. Jacobson said quietly. "You've just had a heart attack."

DeMille sighed. "I know that, Max," he answered. "But look. I'm seventy-three years old. I've lived long enough to know that if this project is going to be my last, so be it. But this is not a normal film. You know that. This is special. This is about the power of God. And if it is meant to be, I will have the strength to finish it."

"All right," Jacobson finally said. "It is a calculated risk, but we'll try to control it with medication. Meanwhile, you have to promise me not to walk upstairs in this apartment more than once a day. You don't walk on the set; you ride in a car or a jeep. If you do all that, then by all means, get out of bed tomorrow."

DeMille solemnly promised to abide by his doctor's orders. The next day, he was back behind the cameras, where he'd spent so much of his life.

With the exterior photography completed, the director and his cast and crew repaired to Hollywood for the indoor scenes. This, of course, included the famous crossing of the Red Sea, in which special-effects men skillfully blended actual footage of the deep-blue waters with model shots.

One other key scene was the worship of the Golden Calf, which took several days to shoot. The Book of Exodus suggests various naked women dancing before the Golden Calf, but in 1955 films couldn't be very specific on that point. Still, DeMille knew how to make it look seductive anyway. At first, the pretty extra girls he'd cast as the principal orgiasts threw themselves into their task with abandon, but by the fourth day their enthusiasm had dissipated somewhat. At last, one of the extra girls went over to the first assistant director. "Tell me, Eddie," she said, "who do you have to sleep with to get off this picture?" It's a famous DeMille story, but it's true—I can vouch for it.

Two important casting decisions remained. One was what DeMille recalled as the "greatest single problem in *The Ten Commandments*"—namely, who would speak the voice of God. A long line of actors was called in for voice tests. Promising voices were recorded, altered, amplified, and reverberated. "We tried everything," said DeMille. "Everything was wrong." Finally, it dawned on him to use the most remarkable voice in the whole picture: Heston's.

DeMille makes no mention of it in his autobiography, but I had actually suggested as much during that first night in St. Catherine's Monastery. In the shadow of Mount Sinai, where would you hear the voice of God, if not inside yourself? When I mentioned the idea, DeMille said wryly, "You know, you've got a pretty good part already." But now, he had agreed to let me do it. And so I read the lines of God, and technicians deepened the sound to make it more distinctive from the voice of Moses.

The only exception was in the pivotal scene in which God hands down the commandments to Moses. Wilcoxon found an actor with the proper voice for these lines, and DeMille agreed

Moses, the shepherd. The staff, which I still have, is considered to be one of the most valuable film props in existence.

to use him. The actor was recorded in strictest secrecy. On DeMille's orders, his name has never been divulged.

There was one more crucial bit of casting—the part of Moses as a little baby, adrift in his basket on the Nile. Before embarking for Egypt, someone had told DeMille that Lydia would not be coming along because she was pregnant. Shortly thereafter, DeMille cornered her at a dinner.

"When is your child due?" he asked.

"Well, early February—the twelfth," Lydia answered.

DeMille did some mental arithmetic, and then said, "Your baby will be three months old when we get to the scene of the baby floating in the Nile."

"That's right, Mr. DeMille."

"If it's a boy," DeMille said, "he can have the part."

On February 12, 1955, Fraser Heston was born. At three o'clock in the morning, Lydia received a telegram from DeMille. It read: CONGRATULATIONS. HE'S CAST IN THE PART. It was to be Fraser's first and only acting role.

"After this difficult performance," explains Lydia, "Fray retired from acting. As a director, he now works on the other side of the camera, sometimes having to make bricks without straw."

How did Lydia feel about seeing her infant son cast off in a not very seaworthy basket? "I was worried," says Lydia, "especially when the basket began to sink." Chuck described the scene.

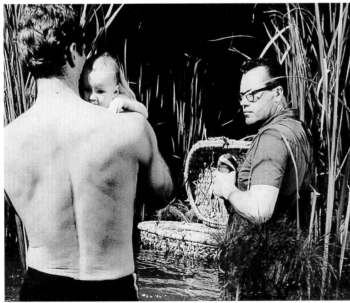

Opposite: Moses casts the tablets down after finding the people of Israel worshipping a golden calf. Left and above: Preparing Fraser for his only screen role. He stayed calm, even when the basket began to sink.

Of course, it was done in a tank that was perhaps four feet deep. The basket floated okay, but it leaked. So before long, it started to sink. Fray didn't seem to mind. He seemed serene. Or looking forward to lunch, since Lydia was on the set in case a little snack was called for.

There was someone there from the labor department, making sure the child was under the lights only for so many minutes, and on the lot for only two hours in a day, and all the other regulations applying to an infant on a film. I was in the water nearby, the vigilant father. So here comes this formidable nurse person carrying my son.

"I'll take him now," I said.

"No, no one can handle him except me," the nurse insisted.

I summoned the voice I had only recently used to face down Pharaoh. "Give me that child," I said softly. She did.

DeMILLE WAS RIGHT. Heston's acting *had* matured, very much to DeMille's taste. Heston doesn't act, he *lives* the character of Moses. Belying his contention that he was young for the part, Heston carries *The Ten Commandments* as few others— even more experienced actors—could have. It is considered, justifiably, his signature performance. Audiences around the world would agree. Even to this day, film fans see him and recall "the man who parted the Red Sea."

The film opened on November 8, 1956, at the Criterion Theater in New York to mostly favorable reviews, and people flocked to see it. What had started as the most expensive film ever made became the biggest blockbuster of the postwar era. By the end of its initial release, Paramount's ticket sales totaled $83.6 million.

DeMille was pleased. *The Ten Commandments* was everything he had hoped it would be. It mattered less that the film was cold-shouldered by the Academy and only won one Oscar, for Special Effects. He knew that it was his masterpiece, the picture he would be remembered by.

He had also filmed it not a moment too soon. As applause filled the Criterion on that rainy November night, tanks were rolling over the very desert ground where, only recently, cameras had stood. Egyptian armored forces clashed with Israeli, French, and British tanks. The Suez Crisis had begun.

My only regret is that today, the post-baby boom generation has only seen it on the small television set. The film was designed to be seen on a wide screen in its full original color and stereo sound effects. TV is simply not the same thing.

Don't get me wrong, though. I'm not complaining. They're still showing it on television every Easter, and I couldn't be happier.

THE GREATEST EVENT IN MOTION PICTURE HISTORY!

Photographs by
Koteh, Ottawa

CECIL B DeMILLE'S
PRODUCTION

THE TEN COMMANDMENTS

STARRING

CHARLTON   YUL   ANNE   EDWARD G.   YVONNE   DEBRA   JOHN
HESTON · BRYNNER · BAXTER · ROBINSON · DE CARLO · PAGET · DEREK

SIR CEDRIC HARDWICKE · NINA FOCH · MARTHA SCOTT · JUDITH ANDERSON · VINCENT PRICE

DIRECTED BY CECIL B. DeMILLE
TECHNICOLOR*

WRITTEN FOR THE SCREEN BY AENEAS MacKENZIE · JESSE L. LASKY, Jr. · JACK GARISS · FREDRIC M. FRANK
Based upon the HOLY SCRIPTURES and other ancient and modern writings PRODUCED BY MOTION PICTURE ASSOCIATES, INC.

VISTAVISION

From WE

Orson deserved better of the film industry than he got; it is also true that the film industry deserved better of Orson than it got.

LLES *to* WYLER

1958 WAS THE YEAR IN WHICH Charlton Heston became a superstar. Before that, he was a respectable Hollywood actor who had already appeared in fifteen films, achieved considerable screen recognition, and received favorable notices. Some of his pictures had done very well at the box office, and his success had provided him with enough savings to keep himself, Lydia, and their young son living very comfortably. He had achieved something that New York actors hardly dared to dream of. But he had not been a *star* before. *The Ten Commandments* made him one.

Heston doesn't like the word very much. "I prefer the idea of a successful actor," he says. But a star he had become. And with that status came a new set of prerogatives: a better choice of scripts, and the leverage to change a script if he saw something he didn't like. A share in the proceeds. And, perhaps most important, a say in who was going to be there with him on the set, both in front of and behind the camera. In his next film, *Touch of Evil*, Heston would put these prerogatives to good use.

Touch of Evil was based on the novel *Badge of Evil*, a police thriller written by Whit Masterson. In 1956, the rights to the book had been purchased by producer Albert Zugsmith, who had been a newspaper man and a television executive before producing films. *Badge of Evil* was not like's Zugsmith usual fare. The plot was more complex than the cut-and-dried story lines that the producer preferred, and riddled with violence. But Zugsmith liked it. He also knew which actor he wanted to play the role of the corrupt cop, but his choice, though a brilliant actor (and director) was somewhat *persona non grata* in the Hollywood community just now: Orson Welles. As a director, Welles had alienated the studios with his undisciplined shooting schedules, high cost overruns, and erratic results. However, he had just appeared in another Zugsmith project, *Man in the Shadow*, which was Welles's first acting role in a Hollywood picture in ten years. Welles had showed up on time and his performance was superb. Consequently, Zugsmith asked him to portray the corrupt police chief, Hank Quinlan, in the new movie. That left the question of who the other lead would be—the police detective. This character was the hero of the story, a man of impeccable moral rectitude, the perfect balance to the corrupting power of Hank Quinlan. Zugsmith had seen *The Ten Commandments* and came away convinced that Charlton Heston was the perfect choice for the role. He asked Universal to send Heston the script so that he could to read it over the Christmas holidays.

THE MAN WHO HAD DEFEATED the on-screen legions of Ramses II was using a plumber's snake to dislodge a diaper from the water lines. The Hestons were spending the holidays at their Michigan home, surrounded by Chuck's beloved birch and pine woods.

On the fourteen-mile return trip to the plumbers' store, I stopped to pick up my mail, and there in the box was the script from Universal—one more to add to the pile I'd taken with me. After supper, I picked it up and started to read, but by page twenty I was fast asleep. The next day I finished it and called Universal.

"It's not a bad script," I said, "but police stories are like Westerns. You guys have been making them for over fifty years, so all the best ideas have already been tried. What it comes down to is, who's the director. Have you decided on anyone yet?"

"Well, ah, no, actually. But we have Orson Welles to play the heavy."

"Well then, why don't you ask him to direct as well? He's a pretty good director, you know."

Above: Lydia and I at our cabin in the woods of Michigan. Opposite: Feeding one of the local residents.

"Him, direct? Well, okay, Citizen Kane *and ah, all that. Interesting. Would be, wouldn't it. Him, directing. The film. Interesting. Mmmm. Gotta get back to you on that."*

The studio very much wanted Heston to take the role. If hiring Orson Welles as a director was the way to get him to accept, then that's the way it was going to be. Zugsmith headed for Universal and argued his case, but the studio was skeptical. Fortunately, some executives came to his aid. Ernest Nimms, head of postproduction, had enjoyed working with Welles on *The Stranger* (1946) and had suggested that Universal give Orson a film to direct. Ed Muhl, head of production, turned to producer Jim Pratt for advice. Pratt, as it turned out, was also an avid fan of Welles. Most important, Universal wanted Heston as much as Zugsmith did.

In the end, Welles got the directing job, and Universal got Heston. It was an impressive display of the new kind of weight that stars such as Heston were beginning to possess.

Still, Universal was wary of Welles. He hadn't directed in Hollywood in ten years, not since the disastrous *The Lady from Shanghai* (1948) had nearly bankrupted Columbia. Shortly thereafter, RKO took the unusual step of repossessing the footage of Welles's unfinished docudrama, *It's All True* (1942), and Orson Welles saw little alternative but to work in Europe and work there in exile.

But Heston had always admired Orson Welles. *It seemed to me, remembering* Kane, *that we had a chance at a great film.* There was chemistry between the two men; no doubt, the love they both had for Shakespeare and the stage was an important factor. However, Heston was the consummate actor, whereas Welles found his true joy in directing.

To get matters on the right track, Welles moved into a house on Chevy Chase Drive in Beverly Hills, and invited Heston to come over and discuss the project.

Welles swung open the door of the house he was renting, and there he was, a looming figure in a flowing black Moorish robe from his Othello. *I was taller, but he filled the room with his voice, his energy—in short, with* himself. *I always found him a fascinating figure: very intelligent, very gifted, and truly witty. As it turned out, he was three days into a rewrite of the entire script, which he finished a day and half later. It was a vast improvement, most interesting to me in that he'd turned my character into a Mexican attorney.*

We decided his name was Vargas, and we continued to invent background details as we went along. He came from a wealthy family, was educated at Harvard, and no doubt destined for a brilliant government career—a man fiercely proud of his Mexican heritage. The problem was that I looked anything but Mexican. Welles sent me to the makeup department, where they died my hair black and darkened my skin. Orson scoured Los Angeles for the best Mexican tailor from whom he ordered me a tailor-made suit.

As for himself, Welles took readily to the evil character of Hank Quinlan. He delighted in the role, and exaggerated Quinlan's corrupt, sleazy traits. François Truffaut, in his foreword to André Bazin's classic critique *Orson Welles: A Critical View*, noted that "Welles made himself look old and ugly as though to demonstrate, through exaggeration, that he has once and for all given up playing youthful leads—even though at this point, in 1957, he was only forty-two."

Welles now had the story in place: Vargas, a Mexican, and his lovely American bride witness a brutal car-bomb murder. Since the explosion occurs on the border between Mexico and the U.S., Vargas offers his assistance to Quinlan, the police chief charged with the investigation. Before long, Vargas is shocked to discover that Quinlan has planted evidence on a Mexican suspect in order to close the case quickly. (With this twist, Welles had a point to make. In 1942, he had come to the defense of seventeen young Mexicans who were wrongly accused of conspiracy to commit murder. The trial ended in guilty verdicts and led to a wave of anti-Mexican sentiment. Welles's fervor of those days is echoed in Vargas's passionate defense of a young Mexican.) In order to get rid of Vargas, Quinlan orchestrates the kidnapping of Vargas's wife and even has her imprisoned. Vargas, now with his back to the wall, secretly tapes a conversation between Quinlan and a crony of his, and gets hard evidence of the cop's corrupt dealings. Quinlan is exposed and dies. Thus, in Welles's hands, the police thriller became a tragedy of Shakespearean proportions, about a moral man forced to use evil to fight an even greater evil.

The two men now turned to casting the other roles.

Our budget of less than a million dollars for the whole film left little money for the actors, but everyone wanted to work in Orson's first film in ten years. Janet Leigh was cast as the female lead. For the manager of the motel, I suggested Dennis Weaver. Long before his "McCloud" television days, he was chiefly known as Chester in the "Gunsmoke" television series. I called Dennis and persuaded him to play a crazy motel-keeper for us. He accepted and gave a wonderfully loony performance.

In creating the character of an innkeeper whose befuddled naïveté is a mere front for a deep-rooted perversity, Weaver foreshadowed the character of Norman Bates in *Psycho*, which Alfred Hitchcock filmed three years later, with the victim once again played by Janet Leigh.

A special treat in the film is the unexpected cameo appearance of Marlene Dietrich as Tanya, the reigning madam of the town. Welles's biographers give conflicting reports as to how she made it into the film. Charles Higham says that she was cast after "considerable negotiation," but according to Barbara Leaming, Welles called her on impulse the night before the planned shooting. "I got this brainstorm," Welles is supposed to have said. "You've got to come to work tomorrow in this movie."

"What should I look like?" asked Dietrich.

"You should be *dark*," he replied. And dark and menacing she was, in a sexy sort of way, muttering the most famous line of the film: "Hank Quinlan, you have no future."

THE STUDIO LIMITED ITS RISK *by keeping a wary eye on Orson. They had reason to worry. I knew that Orson had no intention of making the straightforward thriller that Universal expected. He was going to make the movie he wanted to make—a picture that, for the first time since* Lady from Shanghai, *gave him the means to break new creative ground and continue, in a sense, where* Citizen Kane *left off. But the studio was wrong in suspecting Orson to be extravagant with their money. I know directors who have wasted more money on one picture than Orson spent on all of the films in his career.*

There was bound to be conflict, and soon the studio and Welles clashed on the choice of locations. Welles felt that filming should take place in Tijuana, on the border with Mexico, and argued that he could still stay under budget. Universal dis-

Above: You'd never know that in this still from *Touch of Evil,* Janet Leigh had a cast on her broken arm. Right: Marlene Dietrich asked Orson what she should look like. "You should be *dark*," Orson replied.

agreed. Tijuana was too far for Universal to keep a close tab on him. Welles then decided to shoot the exteriors in Venice, a beach community in West Los Angeles known for its quasi-Venetian architecture. It was a fortunate choice. The setting gave the film a surrealistic character. Welles further exaggerated this effect by shooting most of his Venice scenes at night. The question that remained was, as Howard Thompson of the *New York Times* put it, "Why would Mr. Heston pick the toughest little town in North America for a honeymoon with a nice morsel like Miss Leigh?"

The first couple of days of shooting would be crucial. Orson knew it, as did the studio. On the first day of production, Universal "spies" were out in force, and back at the studio, executives hovered near the telephone. But Orson had anticipated this and was determined to get the studio off his back from the very start.

The Sunday before shooting started, Orson called some of the actors to his house for an undercover rehearsal of the first day's work. The next day, he promptly appeared on the set at 9:00 a.m. and laid out a master shot that pulled through several rooms and involved at least four speaking parts. Lunch came and went, and Welles was still rehearsing. The studio executives began to gather in little knots in corners, worried that not a foot of film had been shot. Finally, at four o'clock, Orson started filming. Two hours later, he wrapped and announced: "Cut! Print the last three takes." Then, with a sly smile, he added: "That's a wrap on this set: we're two days ahead of schedule." The studio people were flabbergasted. Orson had skillfully combined twelve pages of script into a single tracking master shot. Universal was duly impressed; it was also a fine way to shoot the scene.

Orson kept up this good behavior for another three days, at the end of which he announced, "Okay, now that we've taken care of the front office, we'll go head and make our picture!"

I remember a scene in which I'm driving an open convertible down an alley in Venice, doing several pages of dialogue. Welles wanted to shoot this in a car that was actually moving, rather than placing his actors against a projected background of moving traffic, which was the practice at the time. Russ Metty, the cinematographer, rigged the car with lights and stuffed large packs of batteries in the back seat. He then strapped the camera on top of the hood, and ran cables to microphones discreetly hidden in the dashboard. Unfortunately, that left no space for the crew. Orson scratched his head. A helpful assistant came to his aid. "Maybe we should tow the car behind a truck and put the crew on the truck," he offered.

"Nonsense!" Welles said. "These boys can shoot it without a crew."

Sure enough, Mort Mills, who was also acting in the shot, and I were given a crash course in operating the camera. When all was set, I drove down the alley, turned, and flipped the switches. As the camera on the hood began to spool up, Mills yelled

"Speed!" I screamed "Action!" and off we went—acting, driving, and shooting all at the same time. Using an 18mm lens to capture the shot, Welles got exactly the effect he wanted: both characters in the shot while housing lots in the alley fly by like giant sets on rollers, the car missing them by a hair.

The most daunting shot of all, one that would defy all known rules of exterior photography at the time, was the legendary, three-and-a-half-minute opening shot of the film. It was a tracking shot from start to finish. The scene began from a crane shot high above Venice and moved down to Ocean Boulevard and onward toward the beach, all along hitting its action marks (like the time bomb being placed in the trunk of a car), running past extras and actors, hitting the dialogue right on cue. It took us all day to practice, and all night to put it down on film. Finally, everything came together like clockwork, except for the actor who played the border guard. He only had a line or two, but it must have been terrifying for him to see the whole company bearing down on him from a block away. Whenever we got to him, approaching the last few feet of the shot, he'd flub his lines. At last, as dawn began to break in the east, Orson said to him patiently, "All right, let's do it once more. This time, don't talk, just move your lips—we can dub it in later. But whatever you do, please God don't say, 'I'm sorry, Mr. Welles.'" It became the take that's in the movie.

It was technically an amazing shot, almost impossible, given the precise timing that it required not only from Janet and me, the couple in the car, and the passing extras, but most critically of all the boom grip and the camera operator.

"TOUCH OF EVIL WAS A FILM far ahead of its time," Heston rightly declares. It is nothing like the B-movie dramas that Zugsmith had produced before, with their clear delineation of good and evil, and the unambiguous triumph of the moral good. In *Touch of Evil*, the boundaries between the integrity of Vargas and the corruption of Quinlan—indeed, between fantasy and reality—are slowly dissolved.

It was Orson's film, as I'd expected—and Universal perhaps feared. Touch of Evil is not a perfect film, but it is unmistakably Orson Welles. At heart, he was the consummate independent filmmaker who could not suffer the strong control of the studio system. It is accepted wisdom that Orson deserved better of the film industry than he got; it is also true that the film industry deserved better of Orson than it got.

Heston has nothing but good to say about Welles as a director. In this respect, he lived up to Heston's expectations. He also has words of praise for Janet Leigh, who broke her arm just before principal photography began. Welles first wanted her to wear the cast in plain sight (and probably thought of several twists that the injury suggested) but then thought better of it. Instead, he instructed Russ Metty to shoot Leigh in such a manner that her arm would always be somewhat concealed.

Heston himself is superb in one of his finest roles of the 1950s. His talent soared under Welles's gentle direction. There is real screen chemistry between Heston and Leigh, who herself reveled in the freedom that Welles gave his actors.

On April 1, 1958, Welles wrapped the movie. Heston remembers that night: *We were one night over our thirty-day schedule and $31,000 over our $900,000 budget. We decided to celebrate in an all-night coffee shop with ham and eggs, washed down with a bottle of champagne that Orson had stashed away in his trailer for the occasion. I lifted my glass and said, "I think it will be a hell of a picture, Orson."*

Welles nodded and toasted.

"Even though you tried hard to conceal the fact that you had the best part," *I added.*

Welles looked up, then burst out laughing. "You're quite right, my boy. That was stupid of me. Well, now I don't have to worry about it in the cutting room."

Unfortunately, Welles would have plenty of other things to worry about. When the director's cut was played for Universal executives, they were far from happy. The film was too

Left: When I said to Orson, "You gave yourself the best part," he burst out laughing and said, "You're quite right." Above: Vargas embraces Janet Leigh. Three years later, she would meet Norman Bates in Hitchcock's *Psycho*.

unconventional, too unpredictable, too *creative;* in sum, it was everything the studio had feared. The studio ordered that additional scenes be shot to help "clarify" the plot. But Welles was nowhere to be found. The studio called Heston and told him that he was wanted back on the set for some new takes. "Is Welles directing?" he asked. "We don't seem to be able to reach him," was the evasive answer. Heston tracked him down on the Fox lot, but Welles was in no great hurry to return to Universal.

Orson was at his best preparing a film and shooting it, riding a wave of creative and physical energy. He addressed the editing with the same enthusiasm. The last stages of postproduction were another thing. Sandpapering the edit, mixing in the sound and music, grading the prints are all painstaking, repetitive chores. They're also crucial. Orson walked off his own picture. He simply got bored.

That changed in early November, when Heston realized that Universal didn't *want* Welles to shoot the new scenes. "They were upset at him—partly because of the overage on the budget," he wrote in his journal, even though the overage was minor, "and partly because they don't like the way he made the film, I suppose."

Welles offered to do the new scenes for free. Universal refused. Welles was furious and threatened legal action. Heston was ready to back him up. Unfortunately, neither had a legal leg to stand on. Heston's longtime attorney, the talented Leo Ziffren, quietly pointed out that he was legally bound to do any added shots that were needed. In the end, Heston did.

Universal set about to make the final cut. Welles was barred from the editing room. The new scenes with Heston and Leigh added up to no more than one minute in the final cut, which ran a total of 93 minutes.

Little marketing fanfare accompanied the release of *Touch of Evil.* The film struggled through several weeks of modest box-office receipts, and then slowly faded away. The critics, on the other hand, had eagerly awaited the first American picture by Welles in ten years and were largely sympathetic. "Pure Orson Welles," wrote Gerald Weales in the *Hollywood Reporter.* Howard Thompson in the *New York Times* praised the film as an example of "Mr. Welles' . . . obvious but brilliant bag of tricks," and had kind words for the "excellent cast."

Variety's critic disagreed, criticizing the "insufficient orientation and far too little exposition"—which was a fancy way of saying that he was confused by the plot. Welles's "eccentric characterizations," he complained, "are disturbing to the flow of action." But he praised the performances of Heston and Leigh. He wrote of Heston that he "keeps his plight the point of major importance" and gives to the role a "dynamic quality with a touch of Latin personality."

Welles did not receive the instant career rehabilitation he had sought, but over time, *Touch of Evil* accomplished what Welles had hoped: it reinforced his reputation as a highly talented, visionary filmmaker. Charles Higham believes that *Touch of Evil* is one of Welles's best movies. André Bazin called it "a masterwork, despite its detective-story pretext," and particularly noted the rapid pace of the edits, seemingly in rhythm with the constant movement of the characters on the screen." Heston treasures the judgment of *Cahiers du Cinéma*. When the film opened in France, they wrote: "*Touch of Evil* is not a great film, it is beyond question, the best B movie ever made." In January 1998, Universal announced that it would finance a reconstruction of Welles's director's cut, based on his voluminous notes, which have recently been rediscovered.

Such was the art of Orson Welles—the only filmmaker, in the words of Truffaut, "whose style is immediately recognizable after three minutes of film."

HESTON WENT FROM WORKING for Orson Welles, one of the most controversial directors of the time, to William Wyler, one of Hollywood's most beloved and demanding. The two men were very different in many respects. Welles was a prodigal wunderkind who became famous early on; Wyler was a dedicated craftsman who had worked his way up from relative obscurity. Where Welles was mercurial, Wyler was dependable; where Welles was impetuous, Wyler was methodical and deliberate. Both, however, were natural talents; both were determined to mine their creative material to the core and make a picture that was the best it could be.

Wyler was born in Mulhouse, Germany, in 1902 and had emigrated to the United States in 1920. He made a name for himself with such prestigious films as *Dead End* (1937), with Humphrey Bogart, and *Wuthering Heights* (1939), starring Laurence Olivier and Merle Oberon. Two years later, his picture *The Little Foxes*, starring Bette Davis, took the country by storm. After winning two Academy Awards as Best Director, in 1942 and 1946, Wyler went on to make a string of successful pictures, including the charming *Roman Holiday* in 1953, starring an established star, Gregory Peck, and a new discovery, a young Dutch beauty named Audrey Hepburn. Peck and Wyler became close friends.

"We spent holidays together at Sun Valley with our families," Peck recalled. "We were always dining out together. It would be the Wylers at the Pecks or the Pecks at the Wylers." Wyler wanted to make independent films over which he could have full creative control. "Well," Peck said, "why don't we join forces? Together, we have enough Hollywood power to make movies the way we want to." Peck asked his agent, George Chasin, to see what projects were circulating around town at the moment.

"Well," said Chasin, "there is a book treatment I've been sent for Marlon Brando, and I know he hasn't even looked at it. It's based on a book called *The Big Country*." Peck got a hold of the treatment and showed it to Wyler.

"What is it about?" Wyler asked.

"It's a Western. I know United Artists want to get this tied up very quickly."

At this, Wyler began to laugh. Early in his career, he had turned out more than forty two-reel Westerns in the short span of only two years. "Hey," he joked, "tell 'em I've made Westerns in seven days."

Peck was confident that the concept would appeal to his friend Willy. "It was kind of an anti-macho Western," Peck recalled later. "I told Willy I thought there were half a dozen very good parts, so we could do some great casting."

The Big Country (1958) is a story of enmity between two families, the Terrills and the Hannasseys, who both own large herds of cattle and farmland. Neither family has the rights to nearby water wells, which are held by a local schoolmistress, Julie Maragon. Several attempts to persuade Maragon to sell have failed, and the tension between the two clans is palpable. Then, a suitor of the Terrill daughter appears on the scene. He is an Easterner named James McKay (played by Gregory Peck) who believes he can straighten out the problems

Above: William Wyler, arguably the best director of performance in the history of film. Right: Greg Peck producing on the set of *The Big Country*. Opposite: As foreman Steve Leech in *The Big Country*.

between these two Western clans with old-fashioned East Coast savoir-faire. McKay buys the water rights with the intention of granting everyone equal access, but the distrust between the families is too much. Not until the patriarchs of both families are dead does the bloodletting come to an end. The Terrill foreman takes over the farm—and the hand of McKay's former fiancée as well. At its core, *The Big Country* is about man's ambitions made futile by the unforgiving vastness of the land on which he labors. It is also about the futility of bringing Eastern gentility to bear on the unwritten laws of the West, and the futility of violence as a means to an end.

Looking back on it, Heston is glad to have been involved in the project, since the opportunity to do a major Western was fading fast in Hollywood.

The Big Country *was among the last of the big-budget Westerns of the period by a major director. As genres go, these Westerns struck a chord in the American psyche because they touched on the very essence of our national consciousness: the vast open land, the horses, the homestead, the hard life in close*

Above: Two crew members adjust a mike stand. Right: Much to my regret, *The Big Country* was my only picture with Greg Peck.

communion with nature. In the seventies, the Western fell out of favor because its core presumption of American innocence was eroded by Vietnam and Watergate, and as a major feature the Western was not revived until the late 1980s. Willy was intimately familiar with the symbolism of the Western, and he used it to great effect.

The deal was struck. Peck and Wyler would co-produce the film, and United Artists agreed to fund the production in exchange for distribution rights. The two men agreed on how to share the production responsibilities. As the director, Wyler would be the principal creative authority. Peck would take responsibility for casting and screenplay. He also decided to organize the ranch exteriors and the requisite horses, cattle, and handlers. "I had a cattle business," Peck explained, "and grazing land in Santa Barbara, San Luis Obispo, and other places . . . It was part of my life at the time."

Peck proceeded to cast the film. He signed Burl Ives as Rufus Hannassey, the head of the low-life Hannassey clan, and Chuck Connors as his son Buck. Jean Simmons was signed as Julie Maragon, the schoolmistress. For the daughter of Major Terrill, the leading cattle baron in the area, Carroll Baker was cast. Peck suggested that Charles Bickford play the character of Terrill senior. Wyler was doubtful; his experiences with Bickford during the shooting of *Hell's Heroes* (1930) were still fresh in his memory.

Left: Carroll Baker. Above: Burl Ives at work.

"I had a falling out with that guy years ago," Wyler said. "He was stubborn as a mule."

"Well, that's exactly what this character is all about," Peck replied. Peck organized a meeting with Bickford in Wyler's office, and the actor went out of his way to please the director.

"How are you in the saddle these days?" Wyler asked, remembering that that was something he should be concerned about.

"Oh, well," Bickford replied evasively, "you remember how I ride." Wyler didn't. After shooting began, he realized that Bickford could hardly stay on a horse, and an extra had to be hired to replace the actor in all his riding scenes.

Now it was only a month before shooting began, but Peck had still not filled the role of the "heavy," Steve Leech, the temperamental foreman of the Terrill ranch. Finally, he decided to offer it to Heston.

Around that time, I got a call from my agent, Herman Citron. "It's a Western with Gregory Peck. This is a very classy project, Chuck."

True, the script was classy, even though seven writers, including Leon Uris, had labored to make it screen-ready. My only problem was with the part. Greg had the lead, of course, but there were as many as three men's parts better than mine, and the two women's roles were at least as good. I was pretty far down the line here. Don't get me wrong—I'm wasn't trying to be difficult, but I had to look out for my career. Well before Ten Commandments, *I had appeared in most films as the leading man, or at least one of the leading principals in the picture. Now, with the success of* Ten Commandments *behind me, should I take the fourth position in a picture already filled with heavy talent? It just didn't make any sense. "I know what you're saying," I told Herman, "but I'll pass." Herman, a man of unshakeable temperament, did something most unusual. He got mad.*

"Kid," Herman said, "you don't know what the hell you're talking about. You have an offer to work with Gregory Peck for maybe the best director in film, and you're worrying the part *isn't good enough for you? Don't you know actors take parts with Wyler without even reading the damn* script?"

I thought it over and agreed.

With all his stars in the bag, Peck had little trouble securing the budget from Universal. It amounted to $2.8 million—a princely sum for a Western. But Westerns were immensely popular on television, and the recent success of the movies *The Gunfighter* (1950) and *High Noon* (1952) led everyone to believe that with Wyler and an all-star cast, *Big Country* was a guaranteed box-office hit. To further secure its commercial success, United Artists asked that the picture be shot in CinemaScope. Wyler agreed. Already, Peck and Wyler had settled on two locations in California:

I do believe this is what they love to call a star-studded cast. From left: Burl Ives, me (seated below), Alfonso Bedoya, Carroll Baker, Gregory Peck, Jean Simmons, Charles Bickford, and Chuck Connors. William Wyler (at right) has his back to the camera.

Stockton, where an Old West set was built for exteriors, and Red Rock Canyon in the Mojave Desert—the same location Wyler had used in 1929 to shoot *Hell's Heroes*.

THE CATCHWORD FOR *The Big Country* was "big." A big cast. A big screen. A big budget. And a wide, big land to film it in. Unfortunately, the script was big, too. When the two producers accepted the final draft, the screenplay had grown to 170 pages. Here lay the germ of one of the problems that would soon plague the project.

Willy was a brilliant script editor, a function he performed tirelessly on Big Country. *I learned a great deal, watching him scrape every fleck of fat off the dialog in a scene.* But not all of his fellow actors shared his feelings. Many years later, Jean Simmons recalled, "We'd have our lines learned, then receive a rewrite, stay up all night learning the new version, then receive yet another rewrite the following morning. It made the acting damned near impossible."

That's because Wyler was a perfectionist. He was not easily pleased with the performance of his actors, nor did he give them wide latitude in interpreting the character, as a DeMille or a Welles had done. The truth was that Wyler was never quite sure what

potential each scene contained. The only way to find out was to prod and push his actors until they had met, or even surpassed, his vision. Mind you, his actors did very well by him. Wyler's actors have been nominated for Academy Awards more than thirty times, and did in fact win a dozen Oscars. No director ever came close to his record.

No one came in for harsher treatment than Carroll Baker, who played the Terrill girl betrothed to Peck. In one scene, Carroll and my character, who is in love with her, have a serious falling-out, and she tries to hit me with her riding crop. To get as much raw passion out of the scene as he could, Wyler reverted to the oldest trick in the book — giving each of us conflicting directions. First, he took Carroll aside. "Chuck, you know, is a big guy. You won't hurt him," he told her. "Really get mad, and then break loose, so you can hit him."

That done, Willy came over to me. "Now listen, I want you to try to get that crop away from her, and then hold on to her for the rest of the scene. She's a strong girl, so be prepared."

Sure enough, Carroll was mad as hell and swung her crop. I caught it and held on to her wrists for dear life. My fingers were long enough for me to grip both her wrists in one hand. Poor Carroll, trembling with rage, literally spat the rest of her lines at me, twisting like a trapped leopard. Her anger was wonderfully real, and a little scary, which made me angry, too. "Cut!" Wyler yelled. "All right, let's do it again."

We must have done — I don't know — ten takes, easy, on this shot. Carroll has sensitive skin and she was getting welts. Between takes they were putting ice and chamois cloths on her wrists. She was weeping with frustration and anger. At long last, she turned to Willy in desperation. "Chuck won't let me go!" she screamed.

And Wyler, with an innocent look, said, "I don't want him to. I want you to get away by yourself."

As the shooting for The Big Country *rolled on, I realized there were some advantages in not being the main man in the movie for a change. There were several days where I was on standby and Lydia and Fraser came down to the set. Lydia would make pictures while Fray and I went off to discover the "weal West," as my son put it. Meanwhile, I had some time to make sketches of the set, the crew, and the cast, as I often do. Fray would sit next to me, happily scrawling away at his own impression of the scene.*

Left: A few of the cowboys on the set.
Above: Carroll's anger in this scene was wonderfully real, and a little scary, too.

MEANWHILE, BACK AT THE RANCH, all was not well between the two co-producers. Peck felt that when it came to organizing the farm shots, he was the expert. This had been their agreement from the beginning. The scene that called for "thousands of cattle" was no exception. Peck was passionate about this shot. To fill the full width of the screen, he ordered four thousand head of cattle at ten dollars per head *per day*. The price was steep, but Peck refused to compromise.

On the designated day, he saw a modest herd of cattle grazing placidly. At most, it was a couple of hundred head.

"What happened? Where's my cattle?" Peck asked.

"Oh, it will be enough," Wyler said soothingly.

"I thought *this* was to be *my* decision," Greg persisted.

"Yes, but forty thousand dollars—goddammit!" Wyler replied.

With tensions running high, the crew set about to shoot the scene as best as they could. They herded the cattle into one corner, shot that angle, then patiently moved the animals into another sector, and filmed that. The shot took all day.

As shooting continued, it was clear that the mood between the two men had changed. Gregory felt that Wyler had overstepped his bounds. Wyler was convinced that Greg had acted irresponsibly, and that he had no choice but to intervene. Unfortunately, as exterior shooting wound down, the worst was yet to come.

Peck had done a scene with Carroll Baker in a buckboard. Like Heston, he always sat in on the dailies, critiquing his own performance as the takes ran past. At one point, Wyler shot him in close-up, and Peck wasn't happy with it. "When I saw the rushes, I felt I had given a very bad, unthinking performance," he recalled. "There was one close-up in which I felt I looked like an idiot. I knew I could do better, and I mentioned it to Willy about four or five times."

Greg simply felt he could do a better job on his close-up. He asked Willy to do a retake, which is not uncommon for an actor of Greg's stature and reputation, whether he was his partner in the project or not.

When Peck pressed him on it, Wyler said, "Okay, okay. Let's do a rough assembly of the whole scene first. If you're still unhappy with the shot, we'll do it over before we go home." A few days later, Wyler had assembled the scene and showed it to Peck, who still didn't like it, and asked him to schedule the retake, as agreed. The last day dawned, and Peck looked at the worksheet for the day's shooting. He didn't see his retake listed.

"Willy, how come my retake is not on the schedule?" he asked.

"Well, I don't need it, " Wyler said, with a look that brooked no argument. "I'm not gonna do it." Then, in an effort to placate his co-producer, he added: "I can cut around it."

When asked if you can rope a steer, you always say, "Of course." I got pretty good at it.

Above: With co-producer Peck on the set. Right: Ivan W., Willie's first assistant director, was very tough.

"It will only take an hour, two hours," Peck pleaded. "We're here now."

Suddenly, his old friend lost his temper. "I'm sick of hearing about it. I'm not going to do it over. I'm not wasting my time on it."

Heston believes that Peck was in the right: *To him, I think, it was a question of ethics, not art. I agree with him—you have to keep your promises.*

"I think Willy sensed this was not going to be one of his great pictures," Peck recalled later. "We were going over schedule and over budget. What we figured would cost two million eight actually cost four million one. For those days, that was a lot. The stress had gotten to both of us."

On that final day of location shooting, the tensions of the last few weeks, exacerbated by the broiling sun and the primitive accommodations at a nearby motel, came to a boil. The two co-producers glared at each other, neither one ready to give an inch. Finally, Peck stepped back and headed for his trailer. He took off his costume, packed his bags, and drove off.

However, there were still interior scenes to be done, back on the studio lot. Peck appeared on time and said his lines, and Wyler pretended that he wasn't there.

"He'd be six feet away from me, not looking at me," Peck recalled. "He'd direct everyone else in the scenes, except me. But I coped. By that time I was so into the character, I didn't need to be directed. I think I did my best acting in those scenes."

Photography on the picture was wrapped, and the gargantuan task of editing began. The first cut ran well over four hours. Slowly, the picture was pared down to 165 minutes. "Any unsuspecting observer who had ventured into the cutting room," Peck's biographer Michael Freedland wrote, "would have drowned in discarded film littering the floor."

The reviews were mixed. *Time* magazine described the film as a "starkly beautiful, carefully written classic Western." But Bosley Crowther, critic of the *New York Times* and an avowed Wyler fan, begged to differ. The film did not get "beneath the skin of its conventional Western situation and its stock Western characters," Crowther wrote.

Perhaps the most disturbing—and eloquent—feature of *The Big Country* is the distance maintained between the audience and the action, made even more poignant by the unfamiliar sweep of the wide screen. The actors appear puny and insignificant; the viewer becomes a dispassionate observer, rather than an emotional participant in the story. For many critics, this is particularly evident in the climactic scene in which Leech (Heston) has a fistfight with McKay (Peck).

It began as a quarrel and ended in what is still regarded as one of the best bare-knuckle fights on film. We worked through it doggedly, blow by blow, in the stifling August heat of the prairie for two endless days. At one point, Willy ordered the crew to pack up the camera and move back on a ridge, some two hundred yards away. I thought I was hallucinating. I knew enough about lenses to see that we'd be the size of ants on the screen. But that was exactly the effect that William Wyler was after—the futility of human violence, dwarfed by this vast and indifferent land.

"I have never seen any great virtue," Wyler said in one of his last interviews, "in the American tradition of punching a guy on the nose if he said something you didn't like. It only proves who can punch the quickest or the hardest." He paused. "The problem that intrigues me," he said, "is whether people can have faith in a man who doesn't punch."

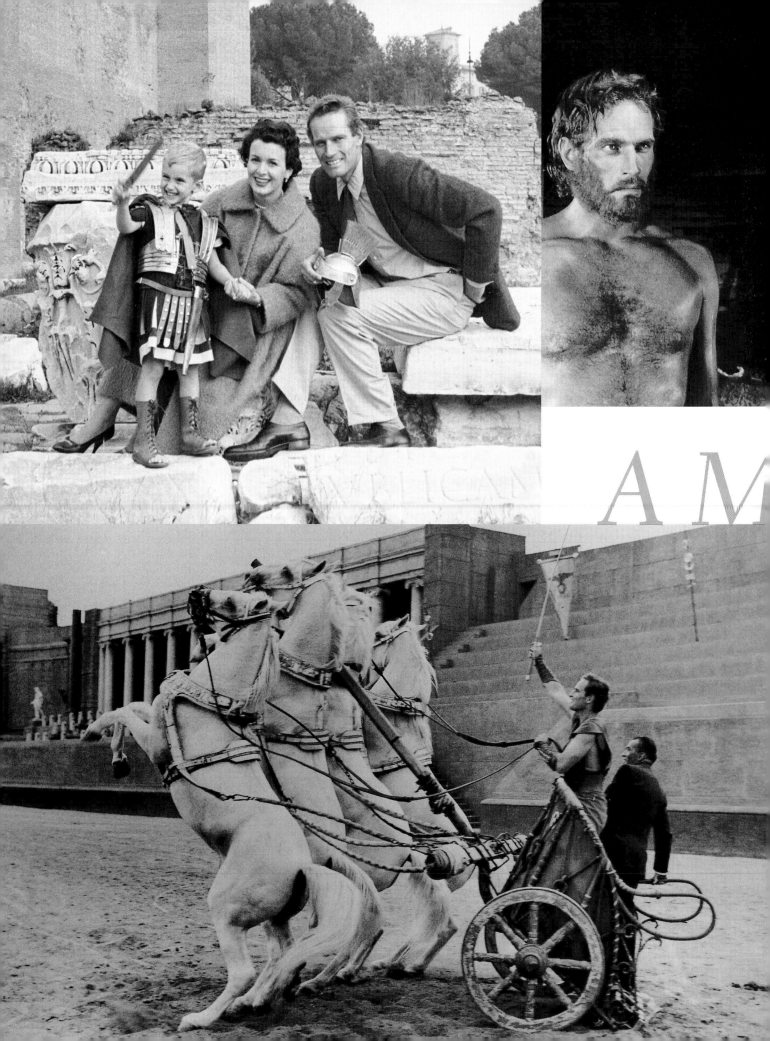

AM

Working for Wyler was like getting the works in a Turkish bath. You damn near drown, but you come out smelling like a rose.

an Called JUDAH

AS THE END OF THE 1950s
neared, most studios looked back on the decade with apprehension. Television had firmly established itself in everyday life; it even began to broadcast in color. At the same time, the hearings of the House Committee on Un-American Activities had polarized the Hollywood creative community. It was a difficult time for the American filmmaking industry, and it showed in the numbers. Throughout the decade, theater attendance dropped steadily. By 1958, annual gross box-office receipts had dropped below the $1 billion mark for the first time since World War II, a far cry from the late 1940s when annual receipts of $1.5 billion were normal. True, a number of wide-screen spectacles had pulled the public away from the television screen and back into the theaters; but epic films like *The Ten Commandments*, *Around the World in 80 Days*, and *The Bridge on the River Kwai*, the three top releases of 1957, were very expensive to make. Increasingly, the fate of a motion-picture studio was determined by one or two very expensive productions. And wide-screen epics were no guarantee of success, as was demonstrated by the disappointing results of King Vidor's *War and Peace* (1956).

On top of it all, the Federal government decided to challenge the core of the old studio system: its inside distribution network. Many studios maintained their own

Above: A happy meeting with Sam Zimbalist and William Wyler, when Willie congratulated himself for picking me.

theater chains, thus guaranteeing a wide release for their in-house productions, but also limiting the public's access to films. On June 5, 1950, the Supreme Court upheld a decision by the Federal Statutory Court ordering 20th Century–Fox, Warners, and Loew's to divest themselves of their theater networks. The decision was a particularly heavy blow for MGM, which had always relied on its Loew's network revenues to buttress its sagging fortunes. MGM was just then embroiled in an ugly power struggle between Louis B. Mayer, the company's general manager since its founding in 1942, and Joseph R. Vogel, a theater manager whom disgruntled shareholders had unexpectedly elevated to the MGM presidency. MGM had been steadily losing money on its operations. Some blamed extravagance on the part of MGM's head of production, Dore Schary. Schary liked big costume dramas, and in 1951 had actually proposed to do a remake of the 1926 MGM blockbuster *Ben-Hur*. MGM producer Sam Zimbalist liked the idea and began to look for a screenplay. But six years later, MGM annual losses had grown to a staggering $5 million. Unless something drastic was done, the studio was heading for bankruptcy. Schary was fired. The boardroom battle raged on.

By the spring of 1957, Vogel feared that a coup d'état was imminent. He urged Sam Zimbalist to see when *Ben-Hur* could be put in production.

"It won't be cheap," Zimbalist warned, knowing Vogel's zeal for cutting costs.

"How much?"

"Ten million," Zimbalist estimated. It was more than double the cost of the original *Ben-Hur*, which had been budgeted at $4 million and earned a gross of $9 million in 1926. But the original had been the biggest box-office success of its day. If Vogel had to stake the future of the studio on one huge gamble, *Ben-Hur* was as good a risk as he was likely to get. Vogel gave the go-ahead.

Zimbalist knew that *Ben-Hur* needed a deft hand. The public had become weary of costume dramas in which characters were little more than cardboard figures. The first thrill of CinemaScope was gone; audiences still wanted to be moved by the story and root for their favorite characters. *Ben-Hur* needed a director who could sustain the human drama without letting it become dwarfed by lavish sets and a cast of thousands—and one who would be disciplined enough to stay on budget and on schedule. For Sam Zimbalist, there was only one such man: William Wyler. Vogel agreed. Unfortunately, Wyler himself did not.

"You're kidding," Willy said.

"No, I'm not," Zimbalist replied.

"I've never done a spectacle before, that's not my style at all."

"That doesn't matter, Willy. The spectacle will take care of itself. What we want, what we're interested in, is good intimate stuff. Intimacy is the meat of the story. Proportionately, the spectacle is, perhaps, one-tenth of the whole film."

Unconvinced, Wyler thought it over, and came back with a counterproposal.

"Okay, I'll just do the chariot race."

"Come off it, Willy," Zimbalist said.

"No, listen. I'm an old Western director. I'd love to do a horse race of this size."

"The chariot race is strictly second-unit stuff."

"I know, but that's what I'd like to do. Pay me what you like, and you don't have to give me any screen credits."

"I want you to direct the entire film."

It took many more months of arguing until Wyler finally came around. One story holds that since Wyler had been a junior assistant on the original MGM production of *Ben-Hur*, he was intrigued with the opportunity to improve on it. Axel Madsen, in his authorized biography of Wyler, speculated that the project stirred some deep-rooted feelings in the Jewish director, particularly in the wake of the 1956 Middle East war. In a way, *Ben-Hur* was the age-old story of Jews fighting for their lives and their freedom. In two thousand years, nothing had changed.

I think what really decided him in the end was the sheer challenge *of it all. He'd made significant films in every other genre—Westerns, social dramas, comedies, cop stories, suspense pieces, period classics. Now he had to see if he could bring off Ben-Hur.*

"The more I thought about it, the more I saw the possibilities," Wyler confessed later. "The tremendous enmity between the hero and villain was nothing new, but here the antagonism grew out of a great childhood friendship. Ben-Hur and Messala had grown up together, and their reunion after many years offered the possibility for a great emotional scene. On the other hand, Ben-Hur and the commander of the Roman fleet started as the bitterest of enemies only to become the best of friends. There was a kind of switch here which intrigued me."

It was not a moment too soon for Joseph Vogel. At a stormy stockholders meeting, Vogel fought off a determined attack by the Mayer faction. After a ten-hour struggle, the MGM shareholders voted their confidence in Vogel's leadership. In the excitement of the hour, Vogel announced that MGM would produce a remake of *Ben-Hur* and make it the biggest, most ambitious film ever undertaken.

A lot was at stake. If the movie failed, it would close MGM. Willy was at risk, too: failure with Ben-Hur, *critically or commercially, would scar even his formidable reputation.*

Ben-Hur was a colossal undertaking. It would become the biggest film in motion-picture history, with the biggest sets, the most expensive action scene, and in 1959, the biggest box-office success ever. It won eleven Academy Awards, a record matched only by the 1998 megahit *Titanic.* It took nine months to film *Ben Hur* entirely on location in and around Rome, where Zimbalist had taken over the Cinecittà Studios. In keeping with the project's reputation for bigness, Wyler was offered the unprecedented sum of $350,000, plus expenses, to direct the feature. Willy also stood to receive eight percent of the gross or three percent of the net—whichever was greater.

As MGM went into high gear, all of Hollywood was abuzz with excitement about the cast. Who would play Messala? And who would play the larger-than-life hero, Judah Ben-Hur? MGM had toyed with the idea of casting Burt Lancaster. Kirk Douglas had read the script and immediately went to Wyler (who had directed him in *Detective Story*) to try to get the part. After *The Vikings* (1958), Douglas had sworn never to appear in another epic period film again—but this was different. This picture was going to make history. However, when Wyler offered him the part of Messala, Douglas was disappointed. He only wanted to play the good guy, so he turned it down, and went on to produce and star in another blockbuster epic, *Spartacus* (1960).

Heston's agent, Herman Citron, had his antennae out all through the summer of 1957. In September, before Wyler had even signed on as director of the project, Citron was approached by MGM. Would Heston consider the role of Messala? "Well, the role of Ben-Hur was infinitely preferable," Citron replied on behalf of his client.

Some time later, I was asked to meet Cecil B. DeMille for lunch. I was once again playing the role of Andrew Jackson, this time in The Buccaneer *opposite Yul Brynner.*

Left and above: *The Buccaneer* was my second shot at playing Jackson. The first was *The President's Lady* in 1953.

The film was produced by DeMille, but the old man had declined to take on the labor of directing; instead, Anthony Quinn had taken the helm in his directorial debut.

It was the first day of shooting, and I met DeMille in the studio commissary. It had been six years since the day I drove by the DeMille Building in my open Packard. Six years in which DeMille, more than anyone, had launched me on my career.

"Have some Madeira," DeMille suggested once the meal plates were taken away. "The bottle is from 1815. That's the year Jackson fought at New Orleans." DeMille lifted his glass and we sipped the delicate wine. "So, I understand William Wyler wants you for Ben-Hur."

"So they tell me," I answered carefully. "But he can't decide which part."

DeMille smiled. "Well, Ben-Hur's the part, of course. You can always get good actors to play bad men. Heroes are harder." I nodded. DeMille paused. "Look, I can call up Mr. Wyler and tell him, but—directors like to make their own choices."

"Willy sure does," I said. DeMille nodded.

We spoke for a while, and then it was time for me to return to the set. As I stood, Mr. DeMille said, "If I were you, I wouldn't worry."

I thanked him for lunch. I should have thanked him for my career. I never saw DeMille again. The legendary director, one of the founding fathers of American cinema, died on January 21, 1959.

Meanwhile, the weeks went by, and still no word from Wyler. On January 15, I wrote in my journal: "As for Ben-Hur, there is nothing approaching a final word on it. Willy is proving the champion decision-avoider in the industry. Very damaging to the ego."

One week later, Wyler made up his mind. Heston was cast to play Ben-Hur. His contract awarded him a fee of two hundred and fifty thousand dollars for thirty weeks of shooting, and a pro-rated fee for any additional shooting after that. After a happy meeting with MGM executives, Chuck and Lydia shared a bottle of champagne and talked happily of what it would be like to spend eight months in glorious Rome.

And glorious it was. By the time the big express train finally rumbled into Rome's Stazione Termini that April day in 1958, MGM publicity people had filled it with nearly a thousand well-wishers. The platform was mobbed with cheering Italians. Little Fray, now three, thought all of Rome had come out to greet him, and he was determined to return the gesture in kind. Waving his cap, he leaned far out of the window and lustily cheered back.

Opposite: As we rolled into Rome, Fray naturally thought the crowds were there to welcome *him*. He leaned out the window and cheered back. Above: On the grounds of the Villa Horti Flaviani outside Rome, a long way from that cold water flat in Hell's Kitchen.

We moved into a palatial estate which MGM had arranged for us, fifteen minutes from the Cinecittà Studios. The estate boasted an acre of formal gardens, a run-down tennis court, and an empty pool. Lydia was enthralled, but I was left with the sobering premonition that with a director like Wyler, I'd have little chance to enjoy it all.

Heston was one of the first to arrive on the set. He had flown in early in order to start his lessons with stunt director Yakima ("Yak") Canutt, a legendary figure who is credited with having invented the job of professional stunt man. Canutt had a simple mission: teach Heston how to handle a four-horse team and chariot, one of the most difficult forms of transportation ever devised by man. Yak had spent the preceding months traveling through Europe to scout for the eight teams of horses, plus backups, that would be needed for the chariot race.

Work started the day after Heston arrived in Rome. By the time Canutt finished with him, Heston knew the subtlest details of handling the rig: *The team I used the most was the steadiest, particularly the near horse, who also had to be the strongest.*

The chariot race—possibly the best action scene ever filmed. And, at over nine minutes, certainly one of the longest.

You see, the wheels on a Roman chariot can't be steered left or right. You have to skid the chariot through a turn. You reign in the near horse, who runs diagonally to his left as a steadying counterweight, and whip up the other three, particularly the "off" horse on the far side, which leads the team through the turn and is therefore always the fastest. A whole turn may take as much as thirty yards and throws up a lot of sand. You have to squint your eyes almost shut to keep the grit out so you can check traffic. In short, the entire maneuver merits your full attention.

But Chuck knew about horses. He had been on horseback in several of his previous pictures, including *The Big Country.* What's more, the actor was in good shape. He soloed the first day.

This is what happened. Yak was standing behind me in the chariot, and after an hour or so of coaching, he said, "All right, let them run now, a full lap." So I slapped the horses on the rumps with the reins, yelled, and off we went. All along, trying hard to control four horses at top speed, I kept asking anxious questions, but Yak answered not a word. I found out why when we came around the last turn. There he was, up in the stand, a critical look in his eyes. He had simply, and quietly, stepped off the chariot the moment I took off.

On April 23, William Wyler flew to Rome to start production, accompanied by Sam Zimbalist. They at once turned their attention to the script which, in the classic phrase, "still needed work."

The problem was the dialogue. The original draft had been written in a style that has often been referred to as "MGM Medieval," with linguistic gems like "Yonder lies the castle of my father. Gladly will he give us welcome." The dialogue of Ben-Hur *had to be accessible to the modern viewer, with enough lyrical power to move the audience. Still, it couldn't be the modern colloquial English of 1950s Hollywood. It was a dilemma that confronts all historical films, and there is no easy answer.*

Just weeks away from principal photography, Wyler imported two writers: the English poet-playwright Christopher Fry and the American novelist Gore Vidal. Vidal proposed a scene with a homosexual subtext between Ben-Hur and Messala to explain the intensity of their enmity. Wyler rejected the idea but told Vidal to submit a redraft of a key scene, in which Messala and Ben-Hur are reunited for the first time as adults. The two actors read the new version in Wyler's presence. It didn't work.

Left: Some of the real charioteers in *Ben-Hur.* Above: Steve Boyd as Messala.

Producer Sam Zimbalist brought in screenwriter Christopher Fry (second from left, next to Willie Wyler). It was a most fortunate decision.

Vidal went home and Christopher Fry undertook the rewrite. It was a very fortunate decision. While Fry did not touch the story structure, he changed the dialogue almost daily, making it accessible to modern ears and yet sound like it hailed from another era. The famous example, often quoted, is the line, "You didn't like the food?" Under Fry's pen, the words became "The meal did not please you?" Fry stayed on till the end.

BEN-HUR IS THE STORY of a Jewish nobleman in Jerusalem, Judah Ben-Hur, who as a young man was a close friend of a Roman, Messala. Over the course of many years, Messala rises through the ranks to become a tribune, second only to the governor of the Roman province of Judea. Messala now returns to Jerusalem with clear orders: to pacify the rebellious area of Judea. Messala tries to enlist his old friend, but Judah refuses. Friends they may be, but in his heart Judah longs for a free Israel. When the new governor rides into Jerusalem and passes the house of Ben-Hur, a few roof tiles crash to the ground, panicking the governor's mount, who is severely injured. Messala decides to set an example of his impartiality and his determination to rule with an iron hand: he condemns his old friend to the slave galleys. On the way to the ship, Judah briefly meets a man who all of Judea is talking about, a man from Nazareth.

Chained to the oars of a Roman battleship, Judah is destined to live out his life as a slave. But after a bitter clash with pirates, Judah escapes and finds himself on a raft with the commander of the Roman fleet. By the time they are rescued, the two men have become friends. Reinstated with his full rank and honors, Judah returns to Jerusalem, only to find his house deserted and his mother, Miriam, and sister, Tirzah, both gone. He confronts Messala, who dares him to a chariot-racing competition in the arena. Judah accepts, and narrowly defeats Messala, who is fatally injured. Near death, Messala tells Judah that his mother and sister are still alive—living as lepers in a remote colony. Judah joins the resistance fighting the Roman oppressors, but Esther, with whom he's in love, wants him to follow the teachings of the man from Nazareth. She urges him to find the leper colony. There, the Ben-Hur family has a tearful reunion, but Tirzah is near death. Judah resolves to take them to Nazareth in the hope that Jesus may cure them, but it is too late: Jesus has already been condemned to death. They witness the Crucifixion, but Jesus has recognized Judah. A sudden storm washes over Golgotha, and when the rain lifts, Miriam and Tirzah are cured and the cross is empty.

Very early on, Willy had decided to cast British actors for all Roman parts. To the American ear, the Queen's English sounds more sophisticated, more archaic—and perhaps more patrician. Wyler had settled on an Irish actor, Stephen Boyd, to play the role of Messala. All Jewish parts were performed by American actors, with the exception of Judah's principal love interest, Esther. For this role, Wyler cast a young Israeli actress, Haya Harareet. With that, we were ready to start shooting.

By far the most challenging scene of the film was the famous chariot race. Under the supervision of MGM production manager Henry Henigson, this army of Italian craftsman had built the biggest and most extensive film sets ever. There was Jerusalem and the Joppa Gate; the Forum Romanum filled with marble and gold; and last but not least, the arena of Antioch, stretching over eighteen acres, its straightaways fifteen hundred feet long. In the center of the arena was an island with four huge statues each thirty feet high. A near-identical arena was built nearby for our training sessions with Yak. The stands held four thousand costumed Roman extras, screaming and yelling with as much fervor as their forebears from antiquity.

Full of people and careening chariots, the experience was staggering. I've worked on just a few sets like that; they can fill you with awe. It is also a danger. Once a giant set like this has been built at huge expense, a director feels a natural temptation to use it for all it's worth. Most directors would have used lots of tracking and crane shots, trying to capture the sheer mass of the set onto the picture. It would also have dwarfed the essence of the story: the bitter rivalry between Ben-Hur and Messala. Willy solved the dilemma with a neat idea.

"You know, it was a really fantastic set," Wyler recalled several years later. "I don't think there's been anything like it since *Intolerance*, Griffith's picture. Originally, the chariots were supposed to come out and stand in line, and then the race was supposed to start. I said, 'No. My God, we must take advantage of this set.' And so I came up with the idea to make them go around once, in formation. That part of it I shot, and it allowed us to show the set in detail."

With his long shots out of the way, Wyler could now concentrate on the two main actors in the heat of battle, using close-up and medium shots only. I think that if you look at the race, there are not more than two cuts lasting about thirty seconds each that show the full set.

Managing the huge set was one problem. Shooting the film was another. When MGM decided that *Ben-Hur* should be shot in the wide-screen format, there was some concern that the great detail lavished on the production would be lost in the CinemaScope process. (Some critics complained that in shots with fine detail, the process reduced the resolving power of the film, making the picture blurry.) The alternative was to shoot a wide-screen picture on wide-screen *film*. MGM agreed and developed a process called MGM Camera 65, which used 65mm film stock. The wide-screen film yielded a picture that was razor-sharp. There was, however, a price

6

JUICER
HOLDING HIS
ARCS IN THE
WIND

Opposite: Yakima Canutt with one of only six MGM 65 cameras in existence shoots the chariot race on the five-acre Arena of Antioch set. Above: A camera operator and, at right, a lighting technician, on the set.

to pay. There were only six cameras of this type in existence. Yakima Canutt and Andrew Marton, the second-unit directors responsible for the chariot race and other action scenes without dialogue, had three at their disposal. Wyler had two. MGM had one reserve camera back in Los Angeles.

"It took an eternity to move them and set up for the next shot, " Wyler recalled. The sheer width of the frame worked well for shooting a five-acre set, but less so when trying to capture the intimacy of two protagonists in dialogue. "You either have a lot of empty space, or you have two people talking and a flock of others surrounding them who have nothing to do with the scene. Your eye wanders just out of curiosity."

Lights had to be moved further away from the actors than gaffers were used to, simply because the roaming eye of the 65mm camera would catch them. Usually, the solution was to turn up the lights, prompting an entry in Heston's journal: "It's very difficult to work staring into the blazing sun, blazing reflectors, and blazing 10-K spots."

Heston recalls that there were only two accidents in the whole shoot: *For one* shot, Yak buried a camera in a shallow pit in the track and ran a team over it. Instead of the wheels straddling the pit, one wheel hit the camera dead-center and wiped out a couple of hundred thousand dollars' worth of camera. Scratch one Camera 65. The cameraman in the pit was shaken but unhurt; one horse of the chariot team suffered a cracked foreleg. Under normal circumstances, the horse would have been put down. But this was a highly trained horse—and a very lucky one. Yak's assistants taped the leg and hung the horse in a sling in a mud bathstall. The animal recovered beautifully and eventually rejoined the race.

The other accident was more serious. In one shot, Ben-Hur's chariot is hurled across the wreck of another one. This scene was carefully prepared by Yak, not in the least because the featured stunt man in the shot was his own son Joe. To have the chariot, horses and all, sail harmlessly over the wreck and land safely back in the sand, Yak had built a shallow ramp. On this, his son trained for days on end.

On the day of the shoot, Joe took the team in beautifully, running flat out, hitting the ramp dead center, clearing the wreck by inches—and flipped head over heels a foot above the chariot. I thought he was a dead man. The chariot weighed half a ton, with steel-rimmed wheels sure to cut him in half, or at least cripple him. But Joe Canutt was quick-witted, with the strength of a leopard. In a fraction of a second, he grabbed the front of the chariot, turned in midair and dropped to a handstand on the centerpole, and flung himself clear of the chariot. Some days later, they ran the dailies for Wyler, and waited for his reaction. They were not disappointed, I can assure you.

"Jee-zuss!" Wyler exclaimed. "We have to use that!"

"Don't see how y'gonna do that," Yak said dryly. "I promised Chuck he'd win this race. I don't believe he can catch that chariot on foot."

They then came up with the idea to write the near-accident into the picture, and to film a new shot—and not one without some hazard, I tell you—in which Ben-Hur perilously climbs back from the crossbar into the chariot. So they put me right smack between the horses, and began to roll. As the horses gained full speed, I climbed back aboard. A scary shot; it scared me, anyway.

Wyler biographer Jan Herman wrote that Marton did not want to show Wyler the dailies of the chariot scene until he had assembled a rough cut with "scratch" sound. Only when this cut was ready, did Marton ask Zimbalist to have Wyler come in for the screening.

"Not today," Zimbalist said.

"Why not?" Marton replied.

"I don't want him to see it when he is drained. Who knows, Wyler might tell us to shoot the race over again."

Marton thought he'd faint. Several days later, Sam Zimbalist

Opposite, top: As you would imagine, Fray had a great time on the set. I pulled oar 41; Fray, I guess, is pulling 41½. Bottom: Chariot rides, 25 cents a lap (family discounts available).

called Marton. "I showed it to Willy this morning," he said. Marton's heart stopped.

"And? What did he say?"

"That it's one of the greatest cinematic achievements he's seen."

Wyler knew when he had something good. The chariot scene of Ben-Hur *has justifiably entered the stuff of legend. It was arguably the best action scene ever filmed. At nine minutes, it is also one of the longest.*

ONE NIGHT, AFTER WE HAD *wrapped for the day, I was about to step into the shower when Willy knocked on my dressing room door. "Sorry to catch you with no pants on," he said when I let him in. "I just wanted to talk to you a minute." I grabbed a towel and poured him a drink. "Chuck," he said abruptly. "I need you to be better in this part."*

"Okay," I said, carefully pouring myself a drink. "What do you need that I'm not giving you?"

"I don't know. If I did, it'd be easy. I'd tell you and you'd do it, but I don't know what it is. All I can say for sure is you've got to be better. I know that's not a lot of help, but I thought I had to tell you." He finished his drink and left. I sat a long time in my dressing room with no pants on, finishing mine.

Then I carried my wound home to Lydia, who stopped the bleeding. Still, for one of the few times in my life, I didn't sleep well that night. Nevertheless, I did get better. I don't know whether Willy decided I needed an energizing jolt of adrenaline, or whether he was just honestly telling me what he saw. In the end, acting's all smoke, anyway. Like Willy, I can't explain it, but I know it happened. I was better.

Then one day, much later in the shoot, I found myself alone with Willy in the bar of the hotel we were staying in. There was no one else around. He walked behind the bar and took out two beers. "It's the simple little scenes that give you the most trouble," he said philosophically.

"This one today sure was a bitch," I chimed in.

Willy drew circles on the bar with his beer glass. "You know," he said, "I really like to be a nice guy. It is easier to be nice, actually."

"Yeah, I know that, Willy."

"The problem is, you can't make good pictures that way."

"I know that, too," I said. "Don't worry, I'm okay. Remember, I'm only an imitation Jew."

He looked up, and began to laugh harder than I've ever seen him laugh.

The days stretched into weeks, and the weeks into months. A steady parade of diplomats, stars, and dignitaries trooped by. There was Bette Davis, Harry Belafonte, Audrey Hepburn, Ed Sullivan (who got to ride in Heston's chariot), Alec Guinness, and Kirk Douglas. For years afterward, diplomats from prime ministers on down would tell Wyler they had met on the set of *Ben-Hur*. Wyler, not having the faintest idea who they were, would nod and say, "Of course."

Ben-Hur was becoming a grueling ordeal, an endless labor of fifteen-hour days, seven days a week. When we shot the galley scene, it was hotter than hell. When Wyler got to the shipwreck scene, the weather had turned. Jack Hawkins, playing Quintus Arrius, and I spent hours in the freezing water. We were six months into an eight-month schedule. The toll was beginning to show.

The medical staff that MGM retained on the set was beginning to worry that some of the principals might not make it. "They had an Italian doctor on the set," said Talli Wyler, the director's wife, "and he began to give people shots that were supposed to make them feel better. He said they were some kind of B-vitamin shots." Wyler got them twice a week. But after the shoot finally wrapped and the injections stopped, he came down with a terrific migraine, which lasted throughout his return to the United States. Talli and many other wives were left to wonder what wonder drug this doctor was giving their men.

Sam Zimbalist was under as much stress as anyone else—perhaps even more. "Willy doesn't waste time, and he doesn't waste money," Chuck wrote in his journal, but the sheer size of the production made cost overruns all but unavoidable. As the end of the production neared, Wyler was fast approaching the $15 million mark. There were no two ways about it: *Ben-Hur* was going to make or break MGM Studios.

Some five months into the shoot, Sam complained of a toothache. "He went to a dentist," said Talli, "who couldn't find anything wrong with his teeth. He went to a neurologist, who also found nothing wrong." Today, doctors can read such signs, but at the time no one thought any more of it.

One night at about six, I was waiting for my next setup when Sam came in. His jaw was acting up again that day. "Looks like another late one, Chuck?" he asked.

"Yeah, I'd say so. Willy's got this close-up with the girl; that'll take some time. Then a setup with me. An hour sure, maybe more."

"Well," Sam said, "I don't want to bother him while he's shooting. Just tell him I stopped in, nothing important."

Zimbalist turned and drove home. The pain in his jaw was excruciating. Back in the studio, I was getting ready for the next shot. The telephone rang. It was Sam's assistant. "Chuck, you have to tell Willy. I can't. Sam's dead." The producer had collapsed on his driveway. It was a massive heart attack. We were all deeply shaken.

"Dear God," Willy said. "You pay the price, don't you?"

Back in Los Angeles, MGM was in a state of panic. Frantic calls went back and forth through the night. As dawn broke, a new arrangement was made. Since the shoot still had nearly a month and a half to go, Wyler would take over Zimbalist's responsibilities. Later, on the set, Willy called for a minute of silence. After that, everyone went back to work.

AT LONG LAST, BEN-HUR wrapped on January 7, 1959. One million feet of film had been exposed. The first cut ran six hours; in the months that followed, it was reduced to four. Meanwhile, MGM put its marketing machine into high gear. In a front-page article in the *Wall Street Journal*, Vogel anticipated costs of three million dollars for advertising and film prints. "Mr. Vogel figures," reported the *Journal*, "that *Ben-Hur* won't begin to make 'any real money' until Loews' receipts from film rentals top $30 million." Later, the break-even point was scaled down to nineteen million: sixteen million for the production and three million for marketing and prints.

Ben-Hur mania swept the nation. There were *Ben-Hur* gowns, swords, helmets, T-shirts, candy bars, and even a miniature arena. Tie-in merchandising was in full swing as the premiere date of November 18, 1959, approached. Someone was offering "Ben Hure" and "Ben Hir" towels. But among some of the participants on the project, trouble was brewing. In view of

Above: The grand premiere. Right: Sneaking in a bit of writing between shoots. Opposite: Fray with Jack Hawkins is a first-century Roman legionnaire, courtesy of wardrobe and props.

Christopher Fry's work on the screenplay, Wyler decided that it was only right to include him in the credits, and secured a verbal okay to do so from the screenwriter of record, Karl Tunberg, who had written the original draft. But when the matter was reviewed by the Writers Guild of America, Tunberg changed his mind. The Guild supported Tunberg (its former president), charging that Fry's contribution had been less than the requisite twenty-five percent.

"I don't know how you measure these things," Wyler said later. "Zimbalist was no longer alive. But I wanted to have some sort of credit for Fry and suggested that his name come in second, or *any* position on the credits."

In the end, the WGA did not give an inch. To this day, only Tunberg is credited as the screenwriter of *Ben-Hur.*

Apart from that, the release of the movie premiered on schedule to ecstatic reviews. "Metro-Goldwyn-Mayer and William Wyler have managed to engineer a remarkably intelligent and engrossing human drama in the new production of *Ben-Hur*," Bosley Crowther wrote. The *Hollywood Reporter*, never a magazine to shy away from hyperbole, declared: "OF GREATER DIMENSION THAN ANY FILM OF OUR TIME." What's more, Vogel's gamble paid off. The film earned more than any other film up to that time. At the time of its reissue in 1969, *Ben-Hur* had brought in $66 million.

On April 4, 1960, at the Academy Awards ceremonies, *Ben-Hur* swept all the key categories and earned an unprecedented eleven Oscars. Actually, *Ben-Hur* was nominated for twelve categories, including Best Screenplay. However, the Academy voters were well aware of the controversy surrounding the Writers Guild decision to withhold credit for Fry, and they denied Tunberg the Oscar. Charlton Heston, however, was the man of the hour.

One of my warmest memories of that Oscar night in 1960 was Jimmy Stewart. He was nominated for Best Actor as well, for one of his better performances in Anatomy of a Murder. *As it happened, we both arrived in the lobby at the same time. The media were delighted to have two nominees at once. We had to pose together, congratulating one another and so on. As we finally turned to go to our seats, Jimmy took my arm. "I hope you win, Chuck," he said. "I really mean that." I don't know of any other actor who could have said such a thing, let alone mean it.*

Several hours later, when Susan Hayward, who had played my wife in The President's Lady, *reached for the envelope, I had a very odd experience. I looked at my left, at a chandelier across the hall, and I heard an almost audible click. I've won, I thought. Moments later, Susan opened the envelope and read my name as Best Actor. I kissed Lydia and ran up to the podium.*

I tried to keep my acceptance speech brief. I thanked Willy Wyler, and did not forget to also acknowledge Christopher Fry. The Writers Guild was furious about that, and later sent a nasty letter. But nothing could dampen the moment.

The ceremony was equally gratifying for Wyler, who won his fourth Oscar as Best Director. After receiving the golden statuette, Wyler moved backstage and promptly ran into Gregory Peck. The two men had not spoken since their fallout on the set of *The Big Country*. On impulse, Peck extended his hand and said with a smile, "Congratulations, Willy." Wyler took his hand and said, "Thanks." He paused. "But I'm still not reshooting that buckboard scene." The men laughed, the ice was broken, and the Pecks and the Wylers were friends once again.

Left: Backstage after receiving the Academy Award for Best Actor, with presenter Susan Hayward. Above: A wonderful moment with Willie Wyler and Mary Zimbalist (Sam's widow).

The

Era of CHANGE

AS THE 1960s DAWNED, THE
American film community began a long process of change that ultimately transformed it into the modern industry of today. The changes affected all of Hollywood, including the studios, its filmmakers, its technical support industry, and its actors. It changed the ways Hollywood made pictures and made money. It created new genres of film and embraced many new techniques and styles. By the end of the decade, the American film industry was very different than it was when the decade had begun.

The foremost changes were felt by the studios. At long last, the so-called studio system was abandoned. In the old days, the studios retained a captive pool of directors, screenwriters, and actors who were used repeatedly over the years to make films that could be relied upon to make money. The studio would initiate productions, cast them, fund them, and release them through its own network of theaters. That had been the way since the beginning of American cinema, and it had served Hollywood well for more than fifty years.

Long before the 1960s, leading stars such as Jimmy Stewart, Gregory Peck, and Charlton Heston had begun to bridle at the exclusive control of the studios, and had wrested several concessions that allowed them to work "outside"—in stage plays, or movies for other companies, or even television. This liberalization gradually spread until a film actor was a free agent, at liberty to pursue whatever opportunities might come his or her way. As the studio system gave way, so too did the process of carefully grooming an actor to stardom. In the future, an actor's breakthrough would depend largely on the box-office momentum of a single film, or two. By the same token, a movie star could also quite easily slip back into relative obscurity if his or her last few films fared poorly. To maintain a career as a star through the decades required talent, stamina, and versatility—and a good agent.

Finally, the very concept of a "studio" changed. Studios had traditionally been the place where a film idea would be conceived and developed, then staged and shot on its sound stages (for interiors) and on the exterior sets constructed on its back lots. By the early '60s, however, the cost of shooting large costume dramas in Los Angeles had become prohibitive. *Ben-Hur* was one of the first great epics to be shot entirely on location abroad, where labor, sets, and talent were less expensive. This trend continued with *El Cid* (1961), which was shot entirely in Spain. Later, when Hollywood abandoned the epic in favor of contemporary adventure films, films were shot on location, European-style, in urban or suburban settings. The back lot fell into disuse.

By the end of the 1960s, when audiences had tired of epics and were ready for different kinds of entertainment, studios began to rely on independent filmmakers to come up with innovative concepts. Studios became brokers: they arranged the funding, laid the groundwork for domestic and international distribution, and negotiated the contracts with the stars.

IN 1960, HOWEVER, the stars were mightily displeased. In fact, they were madder than hell, and they were going to show the studios that, together, they could be a formidable force. On March 7, 1960, the Screen Actors Guild called a strike. The results were devastating. Without acting talent, no film could be made. The lights went off and the sound stages fell silent. Movies in production came to a grinding halt. For the first time since the strike of 1937, Hollywood became a ghost town.

The immediate cause for the strike was the uneasy truce between Hollywood and television, which enabled the studios to make money on films in their archives by licensing—or actually "leasing"—their back catalogues for television broadcast. Until 1960, such leasing arrangements were limited to movies made before 1948. Now, the studios wanted to license *all* their previously released pictures, including their biggest blockbusters of the decade. Unfortunately, the deal was less lucrative for the actors and actresses who had starred in these films. In fact, their share of broadcast proceeds was nil, for the simple reason that the studios did not bother to include them in the licensing deals. Here, still, the old studio mentality was at work: the actors and actresses had appeared in films under contracts that granted the studio the exclusive rights to the films; therefore, the studio could do with the films as it saw fit, and take all the extra profits. The actors didn't see it that way. They believed that television was an entirely new avenue of commercial potential that had never figured in their contracts.

The man who brought the issue to a head and called on his fellow actors and actresses to lay down their costumes and go home was Ronald Reagan. Reagan may never have been a great star in the classic sense, but he was a master politician. Between 1947 and 1952, Reagan had served as president of the Screen Actors Guild with aplomb and distinction. Now, the acting profession turned to Reagan once again to take the helm of the Guild and lead the fight for a fair settlement. "Our contention was," Reagan remembers in his autobiography *Where's the Rest of Me?* "that if a producer wants to use a film in theaters and then sell it to TV, the actor has a right to set a price for the two uses, or even refuse to sell TV rights." The battle lines were drawn, with neither the Guild nor the studios inclined to compromise.

Reagan led the charge, but he needed big-name stars on his side who would not be easily intimidated by the studio bigwigs. He asked Heston to join the SAG board and become an active member of the negotiating committee, and Heston agreed to do it.

I did my best. I was certainly used to being a public man by then, and I wasn't a bad debater. But I realized an important thing—grinding the other side down in argument isn't really the best tactic. What you want is to find common ground. Reagan was very good at this. He could rally the members in the board meetings wonderfully, but his real skills were in the actual negotiations. He was patient, persistent, moderate, and above all, good-humored, even at three in the morning.

Reagan and I spent many a night plotting strategy, making our case, negotiating, waiting for the other side to come up with an offer. At three o'clock in the morning, unshaven and with feet on the table, you get a pretty clear view of a guy. And I saw Ronald Reagan clear in those hours. We had a leader.

In the end, we won. The Guild and the studios agreed on a new contract which not only provided member actors with a share of the proceeds from television sales, but also established badly needed medical insurance and pension plans, to be paid for by the studios. The agreement broke new ground in labor negotiation, and set models that are sought after by other unions to this day.

It is no surprise that Heston's stint at the negotiation table, in those pivotal weeks when so much of Hollywood's future was at stake, was the beginning of his second career, as Hollywood's ambassador-at-large. His commanding presence, his skill at oratory honed by his study of Shakespeare, and his passion for issues that were close to his heart made him an ideal figure to represent his profession offscreen. It also helped that his films had forever established him in the public's mind as the quintessential moral hero. Heston's qualities were not lost on the SAG board, either. At the end of 1961, he became SAG's vice president, and finally took over the presidency in 1963.

When Heston assumed the helm of SAG, another far more volatile issue was gripping the nation—civil rights. Up to that point, SAG had not felt compelled to declare itself one way or another. For many in Hollywood, the nation's growing racial tensions were a problem limited to the South, far from California's borders. Not so for Heston. It may come as a surprise to many young people who know Heston as a committed conservative that in 1961 Heston found himself irrepressibly drawn to the plight of black Americans and the searing discrimination of the Deep South.

I had a close friend, Jolly West, who headed the psychiatry department at the University of Oklahoma. Regarded as one of the city's more distinguished citizens, my pal caused headlines when he marched in a civil-rights demonstration. I was shooting El Cid *in Spain at the time, so I called him up and asked if there was anything I could do. "How 'bout raising a little hell with me?" Jolly said.*

Shortly after I got back to the United States, I went down to Oklahoma City, where they were planning a demonstration against some restaurants that refused to serve black patrons. MGM got word of my plans and was very concerned. Ben-Hur *was still in release. I guess they believed that I might "alienate moviegoers" by my action.*

*"Come on, guys," I said. "*El Cid *isn't going to be in the theaters for another six months.* Ben-Hur's *been playing since 1959; everyone's seen it already anyway.*

NEGOTIATIONS
THIRD STRIKE
CAUCUS IN
ONE DAY

c.heston

SCREEN ACTORS GUILD

7750 Sunset Boulevard/Hollywood, California 90046/876-3030

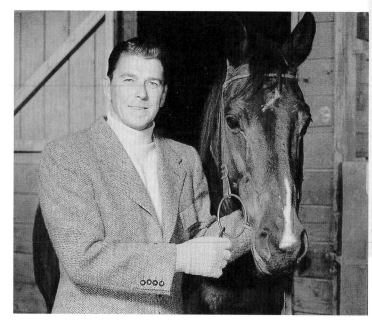

Left: Ronald Reagan during his years as SAG president, and above, at 3 o'clock in the morning during strike negotiations.

Are you telling me people won't go back for a second look because I picket a couple of restaurants?"

They demurred, and I went to Oklahoma and marched in what turned out to be a very peaceful protest. We got what we wanted: massive publicity. More important, the action had its intended effect. When the camera crews had faded away and the restaurants could change their policy without losing face, they did. It was a victory, albeit a small one. It did not have much impact on the growing racial tension in America, nor on the apparent inability of the Kennedy Administration to forcefully move for change.

Two years and several Heston films later, civil rights had grown to become one of the top issues confronting the nation. Heston, now president of SAG, received an invitation from the Reverend Martin Luther King.

He asked whether I had time to join him for breakfast at his hotel. So I went down and we had coffee and toast together.

"Tell me, Mr. Heston," Dr. King said, "is it true that there are no blacks on Hollywood film crews? As president of the Screen Actors Guild, what can you do about that?"

"I'm afraid not much," I replied, and pointed out that whereas SAG had always welcomed black actors, IATSE, the technical union governing camera crews, had very different membership regulations on its books. Applicants were only accepted if their father was already a member. "I'd be glad to speak for SAG at the interguild conference you've called with the studios," I said, "but I don't believe you have much of a chance with IATSE."

Of course, I had seriously underestimated Dr. King's powers of persuasion. That same afternoon, the civil-rights leader met with officials of IATSE. They agreed to change their membership rules, drop the paternity clause, and accept black members.

During our breakfast meeting, King had also talked of a march that would be the culmination of his many years of peaceful protest against racial discrimination. To underscore the nation's grassroots support for his plight, King wanted not only blacks to join, but Americans of every race, religion, and background, including folks from Hollywood. I thought it over and began to spread the word, in the hope of organizing a delegation of Hollywood actors.

We got together a fairly sizeable group. There was Burt Lancaster, Jim Garner, Marlon Brando, Paul Newman, Sidney Poitier, and Harry Belafonte. Still, for all of Hollywood's avowed liberal leanings, you'd be amazed at who begged off. At a meeting at my house, Marlon insisted, "We should chain ourselves to the Lincoln Memorial . . . or lie down in front of the White House and block Pennsylvania Avenue." I said, as leader of the group, "No, Marlon, we won't do that. We live in a country where we have the right to assemble peaceably in redress of grievances. That's the way we are going to do it or I'm not going." That's the way we did it.

In the end, some twenty Hollywood celebrities flew to Washington, D.C. Our mission was simple: to raise as much publicity as we could by the simple act of being there. We were mere extras in that vast mass of marchers, but we had public faces. Our presence had its intended effect.

"I went with Chuck, and it was a very memorable, very moving event," says Lydia. "I wasn't accredited to walk at the head of the march behind Dr. King, so I first snapped some pictures from the balcony of our hotel, and then ran down to join the march somewhere midway, in this near-infinite moving column of people."

The march moved President Kennedy. Later that day, Kennedy met (though only privately) with Dr. King. And finally in 1964, Lyndon B. Johnson, who was far more adept at persuading Congress to enact progressive legislation, got the Civil Rights Act passed and signed it.

THE SUCCESS OF *BEN-HUR* validated the wide-screen epic as a genre of enduring appeal, not just a passing fad to lure viewers away from television. Consequently, by 1960 every major studio was busy developing a major spectacle.

Between 1961 and 1966, Heston starred in six more historical films in addition to two Westerns. In each of the epics, he portrayed a hero of almost legendary proportions and by 1966 was firmly established as one of Hollywood's top actors in the genre. Throughout these years, he never left the upper level of mega-stardom to which *Ben-Hur* had propelled him.

Before I took on the title role in El Cid, *I played the part of a salvage hunter in MGM's* The Wreck of the Mary Deare, *directed by Michael Anderson. I didn't have the lead role but I decided to take the part I was offered, for the same reason I had accepted* Touch of Evil *after the blockbuster success of* Ten Commandments: *it gave me the opportunity to play opposite an actor of consequence. In* Touch of Evil *it had been Orson Welles; in* Mary Deare, *it was Gary Cooper, whom I had always admired.*

Cooper became a star right after his first feature film, as the silent era drew to a close, and became even more important when sound came along. He was the consummate movie star when that title meant a lot more than it does now—the virtual guarantee of a box-office success.

Above: Clarence Jones en route to Washington, August 1963. Opposite: With Burt Lancaster and Harry Belafonte in front of the Lincoln Memorial during Dr. King's March on Washington.

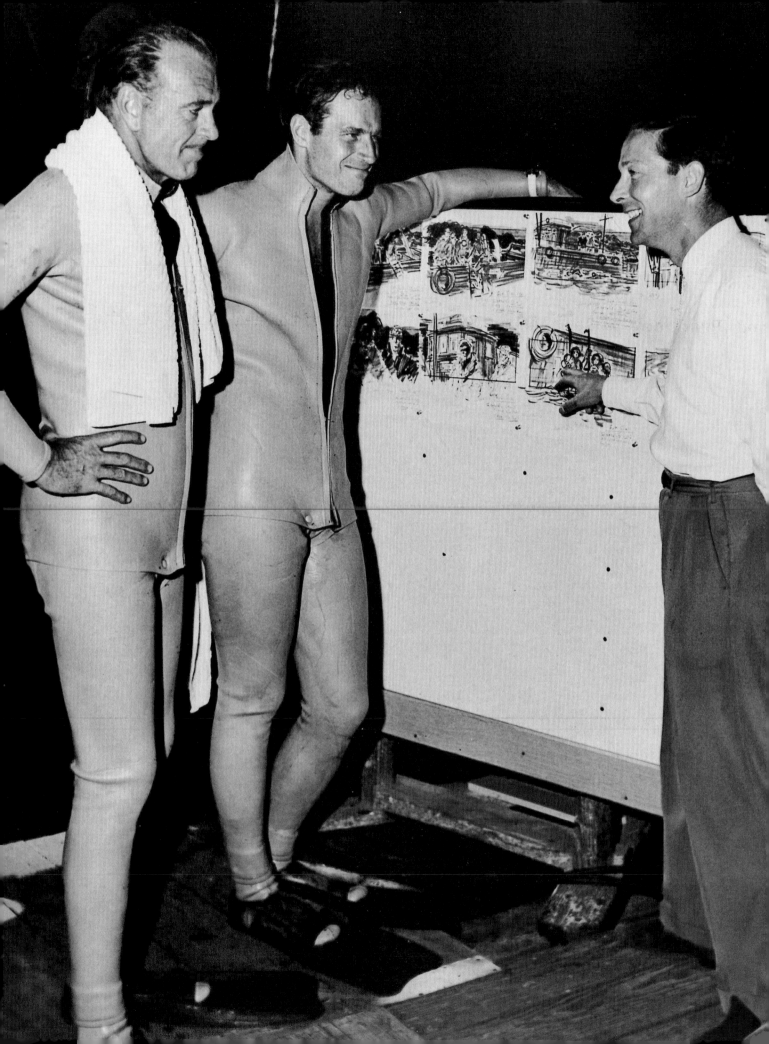

"Coop" was a legendary actor who had far greater talent than he was often given credit for. Within his range he was a wonderful, riveting actor. You could say that, along with Jimmy Stewart and Hank Fonda, he was the iconic image of the American male. He was a rather shy man, as I am myself. Still, unlikely as it seems, we became friends. I found that he could be marvelously funny about old Hollywood, but he was very circumspect in his comments about Marlene Dietrich, Grace Kelly, and other female co-stars whom he had loved onscreen—and possibly offscreen as well.

Cooper made one more picture after *Mary Deare*. It was a thriller called *The Naked Edge* (1961), also directed by Michael Anderson. Before the film could be released, Cooper passed away. It was May 13, 1961, just six days after his sixtieth birthday.

MGM went to extraordinary lengths to accommodate Heston in the filming of *Mary Deare*. As it happened, Heston had received an offer to once again play that most challenging of characters, Macbeth, at a theater in Ann Arbor, Michigan. While he and Lydia were off in Michigan, Anderson adapted the shooting schedule so that the crew could work around Heston's absence. Having had a taste of the old rush he experienced acting in a play, Heston was ready for more of the same, and grabbed the opportunity to do *State of the Union* in Santa Barbara—the same play he and Lydia had staged in Asheville, North Carolina, so many moons ago.

In fact, it was Lydia as much as Chuck who longed to return to the theater, just to keep their life

Opposite: With Coop and director Michael Anderson, discussing how deep the water has to be for the next shot in *The Wreck of the Mary Deare*. Above: Sir Michael Redgrave (standing) introduces damning evidence against Coop in *The Wreck of the Mary Deare*. Right: Gary Cooper had been one of my idols as a kid. I was fortunate to be able to work with him shortly before his death.

from being entirely absorbed by Hollywood. All through these last years, as her husband skyrocketed to the upper stratosphere of filmmaking, she received her fair share of film offers as well. One after the other, she turned them down. But she still accompanied Chuck on his shoots, which would often entail a long separation from little Fray. Just as often, their busy social schedule with worldwide premieres made it impossible for her to commit to an extended shoot. At long last, her agent exclaimed, "Good God, Lydia, make up your mind what you want to do—be an actress or a mother." The choice was as difficult then as it is for working mothers today, but Lydia chose to be by Chuck's and Fraser's side instead of having her own career. Plays were an exception, though. A play usually ran on a short, fixed engagement and required far less rehearsal time—not in the least because many of the plays she and Chuck took on were in their own repertory. It was a pleasure to see how the Hestons enjoyed acting together onstage. It gave their marriage an anchor of personal fulfillment and creative growth that is quite possibly one of the secrets of their long-lasting union.

Samuel Bronston wanted to produce a major epic about the legendary Spanish knight El Cid, and offered Heston the title role. Chuck was not quite ready for another grueling experience like *Ben-Hur*, but he

Above: The triumphal ending to the joust in *El Cid*. Right: With director Tony Mann.

liked the symmetry of following up his two great roles as Moses and Judah Ben-Hur with a role that was a synthesis of both parts. El Cid was a nobleman whose heroic deeds are rooted in fact, yet whose fame is the stuff of popular lore. What's more, Heston was now completely comfortable with the genre.

The greatest pitfall confronting a major epic is the need to cram a great number of characters and events, covering a time span of many years, into a motion picture of three hours or less. Inevitably, the director is too busy relating the great historical developments to spend much time fleshing out his characters. William Wyler was a master at balancing the epic with the human drama. Still, there was no reason to doubt that Anthony Mann, like Wyler a director of Westerns, would not be equally suited to the task.

Born in 1906 as Emil Bundmann, Mann was an aspiring actor who in the 1930s switched to directing for the stage. In 1938 he changed over to filmmaking and by 1939 was working as an assistant director on Preston Sturges's *Sullivan's Travels* (1941). At that time he also changed his name to Anthony Mann. Bronston knew that Mann was a director with a flair for sweeping exterior photography, as well as a careful student of human emotions. Mann had no experience with epics, but Bronston did. He had produced another biblical spectacle, *King of Kings* (1961), directed by Nicholas Ray. That film, like *El Cid* (1961), was shot in Bronston's favorite territory, Spain.

In preparation for my role, I scoured many literary sources: most of the El Cid legend is based on a single elegy, El Cantor del Mio Cid. *The story follows the adventures of a Spanish knight called Rodrigo Diaz de Bivar who was exiled from Spain and briefly allied himself with the Moors. It was the Moors who gave him the honorific* El Cid, *based on the Arabic word for "the Lord,"* sayyid. *El Cid returns and is offered the crown of Spain, but he refuses, presenting it instead to King Alfonso, the man who exiled him. During a final, decisive battle over the Moors, he is killed; but strapped onto his saddle, his lifeless body leads the troops to victory. The Cid is perhaps unique in being one of the outstanding figures of the Middle Ages. Though he never held a rank higher than Knight, he was one of the first people without a royal title to have a decisive influence on history—principally by expelling the Moors from Spain.*

"He was the catalyst that led to the unification of Spain," Lydia adds. "Up to that point, Spain had really been a collection of petty kingdoms."

I had high hopes for the production. Sam planned to assemble as many as seven thousand extras and ordered a complete reconstruction of the original Cathedral of Burgos, to scale. Meanwhile, I was subjected to a new drill: learning to wield a medieval sword. On location in Spain, my day began each morning with a rigorous fencing session. Yakima Canutt was once again present, to stage the complex battle scenes at Valencia.

For the role of El Cid's wife, Chimene, Mann had cast Sophia Loren. Sophia was available for only twelve weeks, so Mann had to front-load all of her scenes in his

schedule. Sophia also asked that her English dialogue be simplified a bit to make it easier on the Italian tongue. The crew and cast raced to get all of her scenes shot before the twelve weeks were up. Sophia was crucial to our project. The more secure she felt the better she would be. Learning English to do so, Sophia was one of maybe half a dozen women who'd become honest-to-God international stars. It was an extraordinary achievement, and she was determined to protect it. Along with the dialogue, she was worried that Bob Krasker's low-key lighting might not show her face to its best advantage. She was wildly wrong about that—I don't think it's possible to photograph Sophia badly—but I understand her anxiety. Now I understand it. At the time, I found it baffling.

Sophia was unfailingly good-humored, though often late on the set. Many actresses are; they have longer hair, makeup, and wardrobe calls, and patch-up in between. There's not a lot you can do about it, except wait. This I did, but with a certain amount of Scots dour, for which I'm sorry. Her beauty was, and still is, quite simply breathtaking. She was quite gutsy, too. We were shooting in the Guadarramas in

Opposite: Researching armor for *El Cid*. Above: Sketching at the bullfights in Madrid, 1960. Right: With Enzo Greco, an Olympic swordsman with a steel wrist. He taught me how to handle an eleventh-century sword. The same company that made the original nine hundred years earlier made the sword we used in the film.

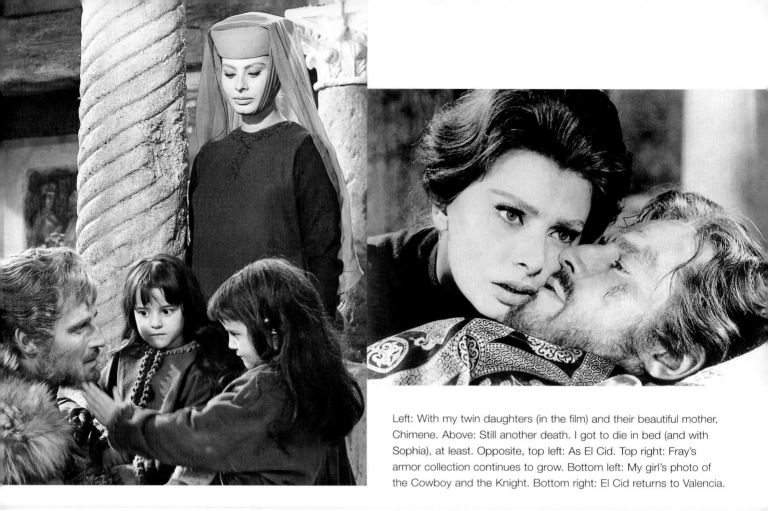

Left: With my twin daughters (in the film) and their beautiful mother, Chimene. Above: Still another death. I got to die in bed (and with Sophia), at least. Opposite, top left: As El Cid. Top right: Fray's armor collection continues to grow. Bottom left: My girl's photo of the Cowboy and the Knight. Bottom right: El Cid returns to Valencia.

December, and we had just filmed this scene in which we had been sleeping overnight in a little shepherd's cabin. Next, we did a farewell scene—"Goodbye, I will always love you," and all that—and she comes out with me to find several hundred mounted horsemen waiting for me. She was wearing only a thin wool dress, long-sleeved to be sure, and it was cold. I was raised in Michigan where we get used to cold weather, but this was something else. We had extras toppling off their horses, numb with cold, but there she was, shivering but not complaining. Finally, I turned to Tony Mann. "This is crazy," I said. "This outside stuff is very tough on Sophia—she comes from Naples, for god's sake. I come from Michigan, and its cold for me! Let's do the rest of it inside." Tony agreed.

In all, I have to say that El Cid *is a missed opportunity. It is a good picture, but it could have been a* great *film if David Lean or William Wyler had directed it. It could have been the best historical epic ever made. When I looked at it again, I see things— many things, in this case—that I would do differently, that I could do better.*

Modern critics, not known for their love of epic spectacle, have praised Heston's role in *El Cid*. "Heston's masculine personality ideally suits the role," wrote one commentator in *Variety*. Derek Elly gave the ultimate accolade when he compared Heston's performance with those of Chuck's idol Laurence Olivier. "It is hard to imagine the film without the towering presence of Heston—surely *the* epic presence," Elly wrote,

"an actor, like Olivier, who plays each role straight down the line, giving a film the necessary conviction to underline the rest of the production."

IN THE MEANTIME, the Heston family had gone through some changes, too. Their beautiful new home in the Hollywood hills, overlooking a dramatic 100-foot drop, provided Chuck and Lydia with an ideal refuge to recover from the hectic pace of travel abroad. And Fray was no longer an only child. On August 15, 1961, the Los Angeles Adoption Institute called with great news: there was a newborn baby girl waiting for them. Two days later, Chuck and Lydia took Holly Ann home, and Fray had a little sister.

"The delights of our completed family and the home where we would raise our children deepened my determination to make it all secure," says Heston. To do so, he delved into the growing pile of scripts that his agent,

Left: With Lydia during the construction of our home on the ridge, 1960. Above: With Holly, my second-best girl.

Herman "The Iceman" Citron, had procured for him. Sam Bronston called, asking Heston to appear in his new picture, *The Fall of the Roman Empire*. It was, predictably, another huge epic, based on the renowned book by Edward Gibbon familiar to anyone raised on the classics. Heston was not swept away by the script. More to the point, after two epic features he was ready to do something different.

Heston had enjoyed doing the light-hearted comedy *The Private War of Major Benson*. So when Paramount proposed a new comedy, *The Pigeon that Took Rome*, written by Mel Shavelson and based on a novel by Donald Downes, Chuck was happy to accept. In the story, an American infantry officer is charged with infiltrating Rome ahead of the U.S. army in order to report what the Germans are up to. To send his reports back to the Americans, the officer is equipped with a cage of homing pigeons. Unfortunately, the hapless pigeons wind up as Easter dinner, and the officer must resort to numerous ploys (including the liberation a cage of "enemy" pigeons) to fulfill his mission.

On October 11, Heston was back in Rome, shooting his second comedy. It was a pleasure for him to be doing a modern story without elaborate sets, cumbersome costumes, and unwieldy weapons. There were no thousands of extras, just the immediate cast and crew, shooting in that fabulous city.

Just then, Darryl Zanuck, who was by then an independent producer, approached me for another project set during World War II. No one could foresee that The Longest Day *would become one of the greatest war classics ever filmed, but I had a hunch. Zanuck offered me the role of Colonel Vandervoort, who drops with his paratroopers of the 82nd Airborne into Sainte-Mère-Eglise on the eve of D-Day. I would have needed some time off the set of* Pigeon, *but I was confident I could swing it. Unfortunately, John Wayne heard of the part too and expressed his interest. Between the Duke and I, there's no contest.*

And so it is Wayne, not Heston, who sits with his broken leg in a wheelbarrow and bellows the famous line, "All right soldier, take me where the war is."

Meanwhile, Bronston was determined to get Heston to play a part in his next big epic. If ancient Rome didn't sound too appealing, why then, he'd make a film about something else, just to humor him. *He sent his associate Phil Yordan to make the pitch. "All right," I said, "what happened to Sam's big epic* The Fall of the Roman Empire?"

"Chuck," Yordan said, "we've put Roman Empire *on hold."*

"Really?"

"Yes. Our next picture is Fifty-five Days at Peking."

"Uh-huh."

"We want you to star in it. We need you to star in it.

"But what about the Roman sets?" I asked, knowing that Bronston had already started to build in Spain.

"We'll use them to build the Great Wall of China," Phil answered, without batting an eye.

I must admit, I was impressed. Besides, doing a film set in turn-of-the-century China sounded interesting. The story dealt with an episode in history rarely covered by Hollywood: the violent "Boxer Rebellion" against the Western occupying powers of Peking.

Heston had the lead role as the American Marine major in charge of the small Peking garrison, together with David Niven as the British ambassador, and Ava Gardner as the wife of a Russian count. Nicholas Ray would direct.

Born in 1922 to a poor North Carolina farmer, Ava Gardner rose to become one of the most beloved screen goddesses of the 1940s and '50s. She was the classic product of the old studio system, carefully groomed for stardom by a succession of diligent producers and even more diligent husbands, including Mickey Rooney and Frank Sinatra. Gardner breathed the sort of dark sensuality that was more European than American.

Heston and Gardner were a poor match almost from the start. Nicholas Ray was ill at ease as well, and treated Gardner with kid gloves. As early as July 1962, Heston and Gardner locked horns over the script, before shooting had even started.

I started this picture with more misgivings than I can remember about a film since I've had any creative controls. Don't get me wrong. Ava was a beautiful actress. Probably the most naturally beautiful of any American actress I can think of. Still, because of her beauty perhaps, she was very insecure about her acting, even though I found her talented.

"She had a small scar that no one would ever have noticed," says Lydia, "but that made her rather self-conscious. She once fell off a horse, I understand. It was a little like a fingernail at her cheek, and she seemed to feel that it destroyed her beauty, when in fact her beauty was quite indestructible."

On the other hand, there was David Niven, whom Heston found to be "a first-class actor and a lovely, funny man to boot." Gregory Peck had said much the same thing when he and Veronica became close friends with the Nivens. Niven and Heston agreed on many things, one of which was the script. It was unusable: *We were in full production, but after two weeks we were still shooting from an unfinished script. Unbelievable.*

In August, Ava started to show up late, then failed to show up at all. In desperation, Ray started to give many of Ava's lines to other actors, which salvaged the schedule somewhat. Naturally, Gardner did not take kindly to this turn of events, and Ray bore the brunt of her anger. "If you can't shoot the leading lady, " Heston mused in his journal, "you're in trouble." Ray began to shoot long shots with a double; he was looking more worried by the day. One day, when a Chinese extra took a snapshot of her, Ava turned and disappeared into her suite, not to emerge again until the next day.

The next morning, we had an early call in order to shoot when it was still cool. I got to the set even earlier to discuss with Nick some options for other scenes, in case we ran into trouble again. All of a sudden, Nick fell unconscious. He had had a massive heart attack. There was no chance of his finishing the film. He ultimately recovered, but his career never did, and he never made a feature again.

The key problem was how to replace him, since David and I still had considerable work ahead of us. Andrew Marton, the second-unit director, was prepared to step in, but I suggested Guy Green, who had directed me in Diamond Head. Guy accepted and flew over, taking no screen credit in deference to the unspoken Hollywood rule that when one director is incapacitated, his replacement remains anonymous. It was a fortunate decision, for it freed Marton to concentrate on the battle scenes, which today still rank as some of the best epic clashes ever filmed.

BACK IN HOLLYWOOD, the film community had its share of setbacks. It lost two of its most beloved screen icons. Marilyn Monroe, the reigning queen of Twentieth Century–Fox and the country's leading sex icon, died of a drug overdose on August 5, 1962. Her last picture was *The Misfits* (1960), directed by John

Left: *55 Days at Peking,* sadly, my only picture with David Niven (left). A lovely man, a wonderful actor, and very funny. Ava Gardner (right) is probably the most naturally beautiful of any American actress I can think of. Also shown are Elizabeth Sellars (left) and Robert Heldman (center). Above: For *55 Days,* Fray acquired another uniform.

Huston. In it, she starred opposite another screen legend, Clark Gable. It was his last picture as well; Gable died on May 13, 1961.

There was a cloud hanging over Hollywood. Box-office receipts continued to drop, and there seemed to be no improvement in sight. In 1961, theaters collected a paltry $921 million, and in 1962, only $903 million. In December 1961, only three new films were put into production—the lowest number in a single month that anyone could remember. By the end of 1962, *Daily Variety* calculated that only 138 movies had been greenlighted, 26 percent less than the previous year, an all-time low. To make matters worse, a good half of all pictures were being shot abroad, where crews and sets were cheaper. The unions were mad. The studios were desperate. Meanwhile, the NAACP was threatening to picket theaters unless the studios hired more black cast and crew members.

At the same time, it seemed that lavish epics were becoming increasingly difficult to handle. *Mutiny on the Bounty,* for which Marlon Brando was paid a record sum of more than one million dollars, was in serious disarray; its director, Carol Reed, was dismissed from the set. Twentieth Century–Fox went into a *second* year of production on another epic, *Cleopatra,* starring Richard Burton and Elizabeth Taylor. *Cleopatra* ran up the unprecedented sum of 30 million dollars before it was finished and the cast and crew could finally move on. Fox faced the very real prospect of imminent bankruptcy, but it was not the only studio in financial trouble. In April 1963, Paramount confessed to its first loss in twenty-seven years.

As if a sign of biblical wrath in those difficult times, a violent firestorm swept through Hollywood and Beverly Hills in November 1961, damaging or destroying the homes of Burt Lancaster, Joan Fontaine, Vincent Price, Alfred Hitchcock, and James Garner. "We were spared damage to our home in the brushfires that ravaged Bel Air last week," Heston wrote in his journal. Meanwhile, other storms of a different sort were gathering on the horizon.

SAM PECKINPAH WAS A relatively young director. In the early 1940s, he terrorized the student body of Fresno High School with his violent temper and drunken brawls until his parents sent him to cool his heels at San Rafael Military School. From there it was but a short step to a stint in the Marines, fighting in the Pacific theater during World War II, where he saw enough violence to last him a lifetime. Although he abhorred violence, in some strange way he was fascinated by what motivated man to commit so much evil. After his release from the Army, Peckinpah became a screenwriter for television and ultimately worked his way up to directing feature films. *Ride the High Country* (1962), his second film, garnished an impressive round of critical praise. Sam Peckinpah was a director with a future, it was generally agreed. This sentiment was shared by Jerry Bresler, one of Columbia Pictures' principal producers. Bresler had come across a script called *Major Dundee*, which deftly wove the story of a cavalry major pursuing a gang of Apaches through the fabric of a greater conflict, the Civil War, and he felt that Peckinpah was the right man to direct it. Columbia gave its approval.

At that time, Bresler was finishing another film called *Diamond Head* (1962), in which Heston had a starring role playing a plantation owner. Pleased with Heston's work, Bresler asked him to have a look at the new script. Heston liked it: *It appealed to me because of the character. Also, for a long time I had wanted to make a picture about the Civil War, which had not been done.* On June 13, 1963, Bresler screened Peckinpah's *Ride the High Country* for him. Heston, duly impressed, phoned Peckinpah from the screening room and told him, "I'd love to work with you."

Major Dundee is the story of a calvary major, Amos Dundee, whose brash action during the Battle of Gettysburg has led to his banishment to Texas, where he now runs a prison for Confederate POWs. Apaches, led by Sierra Chariba, raid a farm, kidnap three white children, and kill a platoon of Dundee's men. Dundee decides to pursue them, but he needs soldiers to do so. Not wanting to ask for reinforcements, he recruits his prisoners, including a former friend and classmate, Captain Ben Tyreen (played by Richard Harris). With this company, Dundee pursues the Apaches into Mexico, bringing the French occupying force up in arms against them. Ultimately, Chariba is captured but Tyreen is killed, sacrificing himself to save Dundee's life.

As *Major Dundee*'s production date neared, the script was still far from complete. Heston and Peckinpah both moved into offices on the Columbia lot to work together on preproduction. It soon became apparent that the director, the star, and the studio all had different ideas about the film. Heston wanted to do a picture about the Civil War, Peckinpah wanted to make a true Western epic about the conflict of men (a *long* epic, complete with an intermission), and Columbia wanted a big-scale cavalry and Indian movie.

Two weeks before production was supposed to start, Bresler told Sam that the studio had changed its mind. Columbia had pledged a budget of three million dollars for a film of three hours in length. This matched what Peckinpah had in mind. Now, instead of a three-hour picture, they wanted a two-hour movie, just short enough to be released on double features. Of course, the studio figured that, consequently, the three million dollar budget would no longer be needed. Bresler told Peckinpah he simply had to cut fifteen days from his production schedule, and somehow to make do with one million dollars less.

"But that's impossible," Peckinpah protested.

"No, we'll work it out," Bresler said. "Leave it to me, I'll take care of it."

He was wrong. Columbia's decision stood.

Sam was an unusual fellah. He was not unlike Orson Welles. They were both mavericks, inclined to disdain the studio and ignore the producer. This got them in a lot of trouble.

On February 5, 1964, production began at last in the vicinity of Durango, Mexico. As the shoot proceeded, tensions mounted. Peckinpah came under severe pressure from Columbia to stay on budget and on schedule, and he turned irritable and difficult. The tensions spilled over onto the cast and crew, and Peckinpah began to fire members of the crew, ultimately dismissing some fifteen people. Finally, the studio sent a delegation to the set.

They would come out to our desert set for lunch, well-rested, well-shaven, picking their way over the rocks in their Italian suits. After delicately discussing our problems and watching a little shooting, they'd go back to the hotel for a nap. We were glad to see them depart for L.A.

Above: With my love interest, the lovely German actress Senta Berger. Right: With our maverick (and gifted) director, Sam Peckinpah.

However, these smiling men in their well-pressed suits had ominous news to deliver back home. Peckinpah was not behind schedule; he had simply ignored Columbia's demand that fifteen days of shooting should be cut. He was busy spending his third million, ultimately incurring a cost overrun of six hundred thousand dollars. The studio was furious and said the two words that studio bosses have hurled at their recalcitrant underlings since the earliest days of Hollywood: "You're fired!" Heston was shocked.

The truth is, you don't replace a director in midstream. I was convinced that Peckinpah was the right man for the picture, much as Orson had been for Touch of Evil. *I argued my case, and even though my contract with Columbia didn't grant me control of the film, the studio relented. Sam could stay. Then, I did something that I would sorely regret. I felt bad, and called the head of Columbia, Mike Frankovich. "Look, Mike," I began, "I know we're facing a considerable overrun on the film. I'd like to offer you my salary to reduce that." To which he replied, "Oh, nonsense, Chuck, don't be silly. We're happy with the way things are going. Thank you, but no thanks."*

I hung up, feeling very pleased with myself for this generous gesture, and not a little relieved that the studio had declined. Herman Citron had no such illusions. "They'll take your money," he warned, "mark my words." And that's exactly what they did. They took my entire fee of three hundred thousand dollars and gladly applied it to the mounting deficit of

Above: Slim Pickins in *Major Dundee.* Right: With Jimmy Coburn and producer Jerry Bresler.

Peckinpah's film. I wound up doing Major Dundee *for free, with not even a share of the gross.*

Sam was grateful, but you couldn't tell from his behavior on the set. If anything, he was under even greater pressure to finish the picture. One afternoon, after a long and hard day of shooting under the unforgiving Mexico sun, Sam looked up and saw it was magic hour—that time when the sun, hovering low on the horizon, casts a golden glow onto the set. "Chuck," Peckinpah said breathlessly, "mount up and take the troop up along that ridge. We just have time to get a magic-hour shot of you leading them down."

I turned and took my men up the ridge. Halfway, I turned and called back: "Do you want me to bring 'em down at a trot or a canter?"

"A trot's fine!" Peckinpah screamed back. "Just get 'em up the ridge. The light's perfect." And it ain't going to last much longer, *I thought.*

My troop was ready. Peckinpah yelled "Action!" and down we came, all at a brisk trot, cast in a red-blood glow by the dying sun.

"Cut!" Peckinpah screamed, frustrated. "Run 'em back up; we've just got light for one more. You gotta be a lot faster than that."

"Okay, but you said I should trot," I said.

"The hell I did," Peckinpah replied furiously. "I said canter, *you stupid prick!"*

That did it. All of a sudden, the tension of the last few weeks, the battle with Columbia, and the heat pushed me over the edge. I turned my horse, lifted my saber, and headed straight for Sam. Peckinpah stood motionless, not believing what he saw, then jumped into the chair of the big boom. "Take me up!!" he screamed. Would I have struck him? I honestly don't know, but I'm glad we never found out. For a moment, everything was quiet; you only heard the panting of the horse. I put my saber back into the scabbard and took a deep breath.

"You want one more . . . at a canter," I said.

"That's right," Peckinpah said carefully.

"Very well," I replied.

Major Dundee rode back up and came down in a flurry of hooves, saber, and cavalry blue. Peckinpah printed the shot, the scene was wrapped, and the two never spoke of the incident again. A few days later, Lydia flew down with Holly and Fray. Their presence was like balm on a throbbing wound.

On April 29, *Major Dundee* wrapped but Columbia had one more unpleasant surprise in store for its director. Peckinpah, as stipulated in his contract, had the director's cut for use in critical screenings and previews. With this in mind, he edited a film that ran two hours and forty-one minutes. "It was possibly the best picture I've made in my life," he reflected later. But the studio announced that it was going to eliminate the advance screenings altogether, which made the director's cut unnecessary. For the next few weeks, Peckinpah sat in agony in the cutting room as his beautifully assembled picture fell to the floor, piece by piece. An astonishing forty-four minutes were removed; some estimates claim it was as much as fifty-five minutes. This included nearly all of the action scenes that Peckinpah had shot in a balletlike slow-motion (an effect he used again in *The Wild Bunch* in 1969). "It was," he later recalled," one of the most painful things that has ever happened in my life."

In the end, all that Heston, Peckinpah, and Columbia could agree on was the title of the picture. *Major Dundee* could have been what *The Wild Bunch* became: a film that lifted the Western to a new level of creative potential. It was not to be. *Major Dundee* was released in April 1965, and came in for heavy criticism. Critics called it "bewildering" and lamented the "poorly edited footage." The reviewers, not knowing what had been going on behind-the-scenes at Columbia, ascribed the film's problems to the shortcomings of its director.

ONE MONTH AFTER *Major Dundee* wrapped, Heston was flying to Rome to shoot *The Agony and the Ecstasy*, his third picture filmed in the eternal city. The studio producing it was Twentieth Century–Fox, which had very nearly self-destructed while making *Cleopatra*, but had miraculously survived. Darryl F. Zanuck, Fox's founder, had ridden the wave of shareholder discontent to regain control of the studio from Spyros Skouras. With *The Agony and the Ecstasy*, he felt, Fox could go a long way toward absorbing the stinging losses of *Cleopatra* and putting the studio back on a solid footing.

On October 9, 1963, Heston read the screenplay by Philip Dunne (based on Irving Stone's novel about Michelangelo, which had sold twelve million copies) and recorded his reaction: "The Michelangelo script strikes me as possibly the best written that's ever been submitted to me. It would be a different part for me, and might be a helluva movie, though whether it can work commercially, I don't know." As time would tell, these were prophetic words.

It is not difficult to understand why Heston liked the part so much. Throughout his career, he has always been attracted to roles of unconventional, solitary men who rise to great deeds by the sheer strength of their character and moral courage—men such as Andrew Jackson, Moses, El Cid, and Judah Ben-Hur. Michelangelo, in Stone's version, was another such man. What's more, Dunne's screenplay did not follow the full biographical scope of the novel, but focused instead on the four years during which Michelangelo painted the ceiling of the Sistine Chapel. As large epics go, it was a curious decision. Spectacles of the sweep and grandeur of *El Cid* or *Ben-Hur* need a compelling story filled with colorful characters and plenty of action to keep the audience spellbound through several hours. Dunne's screenplay essentially reduced the novel to a clash of will between two men, Michelangelo Buonarotti and Pope Julius II, with much of the action focused on the dapple of the brush on *stucco al fresco*. There was a problem there, but neither Fox nor Reed were ready to acknowledge it.

Meanwhile, Fox was busy casting the film. Heston had suggested they engage Fred Zinnemann as the director. He even had hopes of enticing Laurence Olivier to play the part of Pope Julius II, though Fox executives were thinking of Spencer Tracy. "They're certainly prepared to go first cabin on this one," Heston wrote. In the end, Fox's choice fell on the eminent British actor Rex Harrison, who had delivered a widely praised performance as Julius Caesar in *Cleopatra* and would win the 1964 Academy Award for his portrayal of Professor Henry Higgins in *My Fair Lady*. On January 8, 1964, Carol Reed signed on as the director.

Back in Tuscany, it seemed that the financial woes of Fox were thousands of miles away. *The Agony and the Ecstasy* was the most expensive film of 1964, with lavish sets, some four thousand extras, and a budget that would top ten million dollars. Fox had decided to shoot in Todd-AO, the 65mm wide-screen process developed by Mike Todd (Elizabeth Taylor's third husband, who died in 1958 when his private plane crashed). Todd-AO,

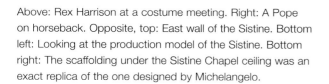

Above: Rex Harrison at a costume meeting. Right: A Pope on horseback. Opposite, top: East wall of the Sistine. Bottom left: Looking at the production model of the Sistine. Bottom right: The scaffolding under the Sistine Chapel ceiling was an exact replica of the one designed by Michelangelo.

EAST WALL OF THE SISTINE
—WITH FRESCOS OF GHIRLANDAIO, ROSELLI,
PERUGINO, ROSELLI - DI COSIMO

7/22/64

however, required massive floodlights, and no one quite knew what the klieg lights would do to the fragile chips of fresco paint.

In principle, we had the Vatican's permission to shoot in the real Sistine Chapel, but when you thought about it, it was impossible. In the first place, the paintings were in terrible shape; we are talking about a time before the great restoration of the frescoes in the 1980s. I was up on a scaffolding within five feet of the ceiling and there were cracks hardly visible from the floor, sixty feet below. You could put your hand in them. Even if the frescoes had been perfect, you could only shoot it in one stage. You can't take the painting off. Instead, they built a complete, full-scale replica of the Sistine Chapel in the Dino de Laurentiis studio in Rome.

"From a photographic point of view," says Lydia, "one particular difficulty was the fact that the ceiling panels are not flat."

Carol Reed had an idea. He said, "There are many millions of people in the world who will never see the original ceiling, but they will see the movie. It has got to be absolutely authentic. Let's photograph the original panels, correct them for color, smoke, and damage, and put these on the ceiling." The color correction was almost exactly what the later restoration ended up with. Putting up those panels also allowed us to depict the ceiling in various stages of completion, starting with the original blue ceiling with golden stars. It worked flawlessly.

Looking at the real frescoes in the Sistine Chapel, up close, gave me the key to understanding the artist. Surely no work of art was ever born out of so much anguish, against such odds. To see what one man, driven by his searing need to spend his talent, did here rebukes all of us who call ourselves artists.

REED STARTED THE SHOOT on location at the Carrara marble quarries several hours north of Rome, the very same spot where Michelangelo had come nearly five hundred years earlier to choose his marble for the tomb of Julius II. Rex Harrison as Pope Julius made a good foil for Heston as Michelangelo, according to Heston: *Rex was kind of a funny guy. He was quite temperamental, but that actually benefited the chemistry between the two of us in our on-screen relationship. He played the angry Pope, the dominant figure, and I was Michelangelo, the iconoclast. It worked out well, even though Reed did not give either of us much guidance as to how he wanted us to perform.*

"I don't think Carol was himself," Harrison wrote in his autobiography. "I think Charlton Heston was absolutely himself, and by the end I didn't know who I was. Pope I knew I was, though the real star was Michelangelo, and Heston very politely and very nicely made me feel that it was extremely kind of me to be supporting him. I did everything I could to make

Taking a close look at the nearly finished ceiling in *Agony*.

myself believe that the picture was about Pope Julius rather than about Michelangelo. In this," Harrison added regretfully, "I was not too successful."

For Heston, playing Michelangelo was sometimes a distinctly uncomfortable experience: *The problem is that you're painting lying down. You're either lying down or sometimes half-standing, half-bending over, and whichever way you do it, you get a crick either in your back or your neck. In that position, you dip the brush in the paint and it runs down on your fingers and drips in your face. It was a rather difficult makeup situation, as you can imagine.*

The shoot wrapped on September 7, 1964; the last take was, appropriately, a shot showing Michelangelo applying the last brushstroke to the ceiling.

The Agony and the Ecstasy was, regrettably, a disappointment. The critics were unusually harsh; some popular periodicals, including *Newsweek* and *Life*, simply savaged the picture. "Phony situations, stereotyped characters, tawdry spectacles," *Life*'s Dorothy Seiberling complained. Even the *New York*

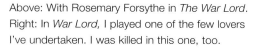

Above: With Rosemary Forsythe in *The War Lord*.
Right: In *War Lord*, I played one of the few lovers I've undertaken. I was killed in this one, too.

Times's Bosley Crowther, often favorably disposed to Heston's work, called the movie "an illustrated lecture on a slow artist at work." Only *Variety* had kind words to say, calling the film "tastefully mounted." The audiences took their cue from the critics: they stayed home.

The movie's poor reception came as a complete surprise to Heston: *I was surprised and shocked by the negative response. I still consider my performance as Michelangelo as one of the finest of my career. Perhaps the subject was at fault; the process by which an art work is created is rarely a compelling subject for those who are neither artists nor those engaged to portray them.*

Lydia comments, "Irving Stone, who wrote the book on which *The Agony and the Ecstasy* is based, said that he really felt that Chuck, who is a rather tall and hefty man, had somehow managed to look small and fragile. I think that was quite a nice epithet."

In more recent years, *Agony* has experienced a reassessment of sorts. It now shows up regularly on the television broadcast schedule, and in 1989 CBS/Fox released a carefully recut version on laser disc, which shows the full width of the picture.

BACK IN LOS ANGELES in the fall of 1964, Heston poured all his energy into the film he had worked for nearly two years to bring to the screen. *The War Lord* was the story of an eleventh-century Norman knight and his love for a young maiden whom, by feudal right, he takes to his bed on her wedding night. Universal was willing to finance it on the condition that it not be shot on location in England but closer to home, in California. Heston turned to his old friend from the "Studio One" days, Frank Schaffner, to direct the picture. Joe Canutt, his favored stunt coordinator, directed the second unit and somehow created impressive-looking battle scenes using only "a handful of extras."

We had a modest budget of under four million dollars, and shooting went smoothly in and around Marysville, in Northern California. We had engaged Russ Metty, the cinematographer of Touch of Evil *who had won an Academy Award for his work on* Spartacus. *I wanted to make a picture that retained the intimacy of its principals against the backdrop of medieval spectacle, and Schaffner had done a great job when he presented his first cut. Unfortunately, Universal was less than happy with it, particularly with the second-unit scenes. Perhaps the studio was expecting another "Charlton Heston Epic."*

Regardless, *The War Lord* remains a deeply compelling film that, to modern eyes, has aged much more gracefully than other films of the period. Part of the reason, no doubt, is that Metty did not try to go after the gaudy Technicolor look so beloved by studios in the 1960s, but used plenty of filters and gels to cast a rich and seductive tone over the picture, making it truly timeless.

THE LAST THING I WANTED *to do was immerse myself in yet another epic. But from 1963 onward I received nibbles about* Khartoum, *which chronicled the heroic stand of the British General Charles Gordon against an overwhelming Muslim rebel force led by a self-proclaimed* Mahdi *(which in Arabic means "the expected one"). Gordon was an eccentric military genius who defied the British establishment and yet galvanized the nation with his heroic last stand in the Sudan. When I read the script by Robert Ardrey, it was one of the two or three best scripts I had ever read.*

I had often suggested parts to Laurence Olivier, and projects for him to direct. Larry was deeply immersed in running the National Theatre and was booked to do Othello, but promised to squeeze in a few days to appear as the Mahdi. The distinguished Ralph Richardson was cast as Prime Minister Gladstone. In addition, we once again engaged Yak Canutt to direct the battle scenes, with his son Joe acting as his assistant.

Khartoum *combines the exotic flair and romantic sweep of* Lawrence of Arabia *with the dramatic confrontation of a Shake-speare play. In addition, it has the poignant resonance of* The Ten Commandments, *not in the*

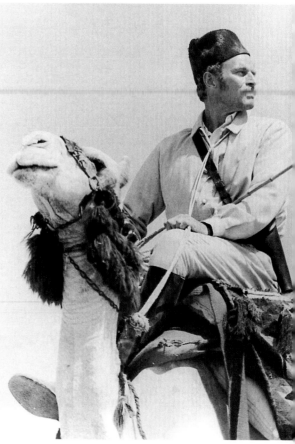

Left: A scene with Laurence Olivier, the greatest actor of our time. Above: Another camel, probably planning to bite me on the knee. Opposite: I hate camels—except when taking Holly and Fraser on a tour of the pyramids.

least because *Khartoum* was shot on location in Egypt. In the scene in which General Gordon disembarks from the Nile to take command of the garrison and the fight against the Muslim insurrection, a vast crowd of Sudanese engulfs him, chanting *"Gor-don! Gor-don!"* in much the same way as a crowd of Arabs cried *"Moussa! Moussa!"* some ten years earlier.

It was one of those scenes, you know. Every so often you do a scene in a movie in which you don't need to act, for it acts itself. It's like El Cid taking Valencia or Moses leading the Israelites out of bondage. If you're in that situation and you hear thousands of people shouting, it plays itself. It was very moving for me.

Heston positively glows in the role. Part of the reason, no doubt, was that he saw himself surrounded by British actors, with whom he has often felt greater affinity than with Americans. At his core, Heston is an actor in the Shakespearean mold. His films have always found a warm welcome in England; to this day he is revered by the British as the consummate actor's actor. Filming *Khartoum* in this company of men

was a unmitigated pleasure, especially compared to the difficult months of working on *Major Dundee* and *Peking*.

When Gordon was appointed governor-general of the Sudan, a title the British invented to give him the authority to rule the Sudan, they designed a special tunic for him, covered with solid braid, real gold. The whole tunic weighed about six pounds. It was made by one of the oldest costume houses in England, a long-time maker and purveyor of military uniforms. When I went to have the fitting, I said to this old tailor, "I've seen a photograph of Gordon in that tunic. It's amazing how well you've copied it from just this photograph." "Oh, it wasn't very difficult, sir," the tailor replied. "You see, we actually made the original for General Gordon. I used the same patterns."

The exterior battle scenes as well as Gordon's arrival in Khartoum were shot in Egypt, and gave Heston the opportunity to climb the Pyramid of Cheops with Lydia and Fray. Meanwhile, Laurence Olivier found out that his wife, Joan Plowright, was pregnant, and declined to come to Egypt. When the company returned to London for the interiors, Heston and Olivier filmed the scene of the one encounter in the movie between the two men. Olivier used the same makeup he had applied for *Othello* and appeared as a dark and menacing warrior, speaking his lines with a careful Sudanese accent.

Appearing in *Khartoum*, Olivier declared in his autobiography *On Acting*, "recharged my spirits—and my bank account." Indeed, Olivier was paid £250,000 for eight days of work in the Pinewood Studios—in 1965, the equivalent of more than half a million dollars. "In epic pictures there's not much time for deep characterization—sometimes the dialogue can be anybody's," Olivier said, "and you have to rely very strongly on the pictorial effect." This Olivier did, invoking some of the effects he had developed for *Othello*. Still, Olivier felt that Heston, playing Gordon, "acted me off the screen—not from want of trying on my part."

Perhaps predictably, *Khartoum* was very well received in England and in Europe, but Olivier's performance came under fire. "Sir Laurence could act rings around Mr. Heston at the National Theatre, but here, as in that earlier and apparently just as unfair contest between Sir Laurence and Marilyn Monroe in *The Prince and the Showgirl*, there remains no doubt either about whose shadow has more substance on the silver screen," wrote the critic in the *Times* of London, echoing much of what Olivier confessed himself.

Despite its international success, the film did poorly in the United States. Perhaps the Great Era of the Epics had come to an end after all.

As General Gordon, steaming down the Nile to take up his command in Khartoum.

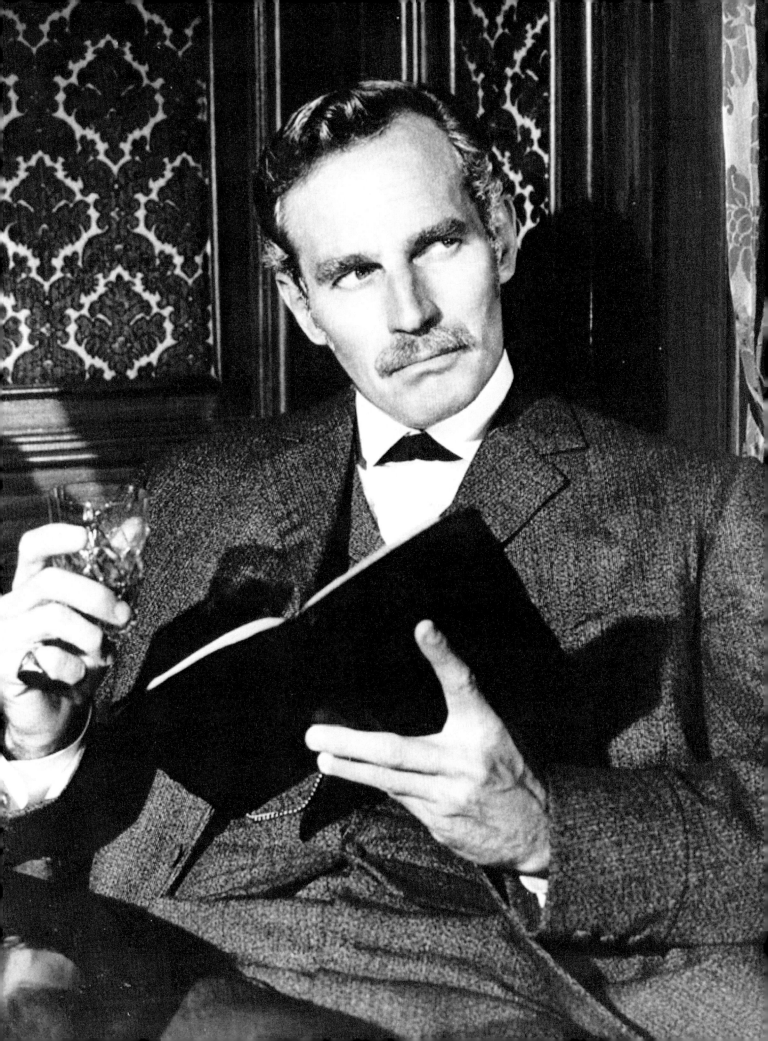

The Age of

Who would believe a story of a bunch of apes running a civilized society in which men, not beasts, are the animals?

ADVENTURES

Charlton Heston fixed his eyes on his agent.

"Herman," said Chuck, "have I become too strongly identified with large, highly commercial films?"

"No," said Herman Citron. "Nonsense."

Heston wasn't so sure. The last few films had not been successful. "The notices on *The Agony and the Ecstasy* and what happened to *War Lord* certainly amounted to two swift kicks in the balls," Heston penned in his diary on New Year's Eve, 1965. It was a moment of soul-searching for Chuck, trying to define where he wanted his career to take him in the years to come. Chuck straightened up and looked his agent in the eye, and said, "I'd like to try something different for the next one."

Though neither suspected it, it was a pivotal moment in the actor's career. The great string of period films, in which Heston had excelled as the pre-eminent epic hero, had come to an end. He was looking at a future in much the same manner as all of Hollywood, not quite knowing what was beyond the horizon, just having the gut feel that it had to be *something different.*

Critics have written volumes on what inspired Hollywood, in the mid-1960s, to change gears and initiate a series of films of startling originality. The wide-screen epic had run its course, *Cleopatra* (1963) and the aptly named *Fall of the Roman Empire* (1964) being the last in a series that began with *The Robe* some twelve years before. In fact, *Khartoum* (1966) was the very last wide-screen drama for some time to come. Hollywood and its audience were ready for something new. But what?

Part of the answer would come from movements in Europe. European filmmakers had taken their work out of the studio and onto the street. They started to make films about real-life subjects, with people in real-life locations such as bars, offices, and train stations. The French called this new breed of contemporary films "*la Nouvelle Vague*"—the "New Wave." A number of technological breakthroughs facilitated this new genre. In 1960, the development of the Nagra quarter-inch portable sound recorder enabled a small, mobile crew to record synchronous sound on exterior shoots. Shortly before, the French camera manufacturer Éclair introduced a small 16mm camera that could be carried around on "sticks" (a tripod), and could even be used in hand-held shots. The sudden mobility of motion picture-equipment encouraged the shooting of improvised scenes, inspired by the chance of the moment. Some hundred years ago, artists who left their studios to paint the modern environment were called Impressionists; now, they were called *auteurs* (authors)—filmmakers who wrote their own screenplays, directed their cast, and edited their films, often doubling as producers on the side. In filming the contemporary world these "authors"—filmmakers such as Jean-Luc Godard, Claude Chabrol, François Truffaut, and Alain Resnais—also pushed the boundaries of what was permissible to present on film in terms of language, violence, and sex.

American filmmakers were intrigued by the daring originality of New Wave films. For years, Hollywood had abided by the Production Code, a silent, unwritten law which put severe limits on the extent to which directors could avail themselves of language, nudity, or violence. Then, in the 1960s, they took a cue from their European colleagues and gradually abandoned the Production Code. In 1967, Arthur Penn's *Bonnie and Clyde* set a new standard of violence in motion pictures, as did Sam Peckinpah's *The Wild Bunch* of 1969. Mike Nichols's *Who's Afraid of Virginia Woolf* (1966) freely explored sexual intimacy and marital infidelity, two subjects only obliquely referred to in previous Hollywood films.

Between 1966 and 1976, Heston starred in twenty films, only three of which were situated in the distant past. Two of these, *Julius Caesar* and *Antony and Cleopatra*, were based on Shakespeare plays, and the third, *The Three Musketeers*, was more of a period comedy than a historic epic. Most important, Heston was now playing men of the here and now, as human and fallible as the rest of us: an airline pilot, a quarterback, an astronaut, a conductor, an architect, a police detective. Chuck had ceased to be the classic, square-jawed protagonist. He had become an action hero.

In this remarkable transformation, Heston did not limit himself to one genre alone. In his role as the hapless astronaut marooned on a planet of apes, he launched the revival of that most successful of modern genres, the science-fiction opera. He sustained his commanding presence in science fiction with *The Omega Man* (1971) and *Soylent Green* (1973), both of which have long since become cult favorites. At the same time, he proved himself in another genre, the New Western. Partly because of the great success of Western serials such as "Gunsmoke" on television, Hollywood returned to the Western, yet with a certain neo-realism that showed cowboys and cowgirls as the salt-of-the-earth figures they were, while treating Indians with a measure of dignity and realism. *Major Dundee* had been an important precursor of the New Western; Heston followed it up with *Will Penny* (1968), one year before the most celebrated Western of its time, *Butch Cassidy and the Sundance Kid*. He would once again return to a Western-type role in *The Last Hard Men* (1976) and *The Mountain Men* (1980). Finally, in *Skyjacked* (1972), *Earthquake* (1974), and *Airport 1975* (1974), Chuck carved out a new role as action-adventure's leading man. Few actors could have made the transition from epic to contemporary films in such a short time with such success. Fewer still would be able to hold their own in such a wide variety of genres.

IN HINDSIGHT, IT WAS SYMBOLIC that Chuck entered this phase of contemporary films with a visit to a place that dominated public debate in contemporary America: Vietnam. In 1961, when civil rights was the predominant issue on the nation's agenda, he had been one of the first Hollywood actors to throw his support behind the peaceful protests led by a black minister named Martin Luther King. Now, five years later, he was equally drawn to the conflict that, by the early months of 1966, had cost the lives of 6,664 Americans and had left more than 30,000 wounded. As the year drew to a close, the U.S. would have over 400,000 troops in Vietnam.

Why did I go to Vietnam? To be quite frank, I don't remember. My journals don't give a clue. I had served in my "own" war, back in the 1940s. Herman had lined up three new pictures, but none of them gave any indication of going into production any time soon. Maybe I was ready for a hiatus of sorts, just all acted out for once. Then again, there was simply something that drew me to that place. I just knew I had to go.

Hollywood entertainers have a fine tradition of flying to theaters of war to entertain the troops and inject a healthy dose of morale, but Heston realized that there was little he could do without a Bob Hope–style traveling band and a chorus line of pretty girls.

The thing with such large entertainment units, however, is that logistics simply prohibit the traveling shows from going anywhere but the big bases, where as many troops as possible could be reached. Even very small units couldn't be sent very far into the field, particularly if they included women. Since I could travel both light and alone, I was able to go to fairly remote areas. Though I am sure they'd rather have seen Bob Hope and the girl singers, at least I was able to let some of the men in the boondocks know they weren't forgotten.

Arriving in Saigon on January 15, 1966, Heston took a military flight to Danang, and almost didn't make it when the flaps failed upon takeoff. From there, he took off for the north, joining the Special Forces on active missions.

I spent my time with Seabees and marines today, some of them in an advanced field hospital, badly shot up. I'll remember them . . . lying loose on the bloody stretchers,

Opposite: In Vietnam with our troops, 1966.
Above: Riding shotgun in a chopper 3,000
feet over Dong Trei. Center: A Japanese
correspondent with five cameras waits for a
ride at Pleiku airstrip. Right: A marine gunner
on a VH34 chopper out of Danang.

*red dust on their boots, carried lurching along the muddy buckboards from the helipad
to the surgical tent. I slept at a marine airstrip.*

Five days later, Chuck scrambled aboard a Special Forces Huey gunship and
headed for an area north of Pleiku that the Vietcong were thought to be occupying.
From there, he trekked further north and spent a few days in Montagnard country.

*The Montagnards are a primitive, fierce, and fascinating people, not Vietnamese.
While I was there, I was initiated into the tribe. The key to the ceremony was drinking
a mixture of rice wine and blood from a bullock that had just been brained on the spot.
This constituted a gastronomic test only equaled in my experience of eating the eyeball
of a sheep off the point of a Bedouin dagger while shooting* The Ten Commandments.
*The Special Forces major who was with me, noting my distress, said encouragingly,
"The blood's not so bad, it's that goddamn rice wine they mix with it. It'll give ya the
runs sure as hell." And, as I found out to my discomfort, it sure as hell did.*

Heston was not the only actor to leave the relative safety of the main bases—
Jimmy Stewart flew on a bombing mission over Cambodia before his son Ronald was
killed in the war—but he was probably the only actor to move deep in-country and
see the war from up close.

BACK HOME, HESTON'S TIME was increasingly absorbed by his duties as president of the Screen Actors Guild, which was embroiled in intense negotiations with Hollywood's producers for a new contract. He was asked to join the National Endowment for the Arts, a position in which he exerted considerable influence in the way American taxpayers' money was spent to fund national arts and education projects, and became involved in the foundation of a national academy devoted to promoting the art of cinema, which ultimately became the American Film Institute.

One day, he found himself in Washington, D.C., exhausted, having just thrown his support behind a federal program to fight poverty and boost American education. On his return trip to Los Angeles, he decided he would stop in Detroit and visit his father, Russ. His father had suffered a number of strokes and was in poor health. "Russ looks better than when I was here last, but still, very feeble," he wrote in his journals. "He had an attack during the evening which set him back and shook us all. I still hope he can come out for Christmas." There was a sense of foreboding in the air. "I feel sad and desperate," Chuck wrote. The next day, as his plane was heading back to Los Angeles, his father died. "I must have known he couldn't live long when I saw him sit with drooping head at his own table and shuffle with painful care from room to room. Still . . . to have him dead is hard and hurtful. Not for him. He was ready, I think, but I'm not. I remember him strong and taller than I.

"Life goes on," he reflected, "like a stream flowing at the same speed, over the same bed as before, making only a ripple or two over the rock that's dropped into it."

IT SEEMED TO ME CLEARLY the basis for a film. A new genre, the space opera. Some say it was a better story than any of them, about this withdrawn misanthropic astronaut who finds himself on a planet ruled by an ape society, and is called upon to defend humanity.

It was the Darwinian evolution theory put on its head, and it became a smash box-office success. It was *Planet of the Apes*. The idea for the film had come from a young and very determined producer named Arthur Jacobs, who had acquired the rights to a French novel called *La Planète des Singes*. It was written by Pierre Boulle, who was also responsible for the screenplay for *The Bridge on the River Kwai* (1957).

The basic problem was the premise. Who would believe a story of a bunch of apes running a civilized society in which men, not beasts, are the animals?

Studios said, come on now, you're talking about Buck Rogers in the twenty-fifth century, Saturday morning matinee stuff. Science fiction was not yet a recognized genre for mature feature films. The other problem was the cost; it was putting many studios off. When the project came across the desk of Richard Zanuck at Fox, Dick put his finger on the heart of the matter. He looked at the paintings and the storyboards and said, "These are not going to be real apes, right? These are going to be actors in ape costumes and makeup, right?"

"Well, of course," we said.

Zanuck turned away from the storyboards. "What if they laugh at the makeups?"

"If they laugh at the makeups, it's bye-bye."

"I tell you what," Zanuck continued. "I'll put up fifty thousand dollars to develop the makeup, and we'll do a test."

The makeup artists were led by John Chambers, who later crafted the ears for Leonard Nimoy's Mr. Spock on "Star Trek." The masks they created had a realism and flexibility that was unprecedented. The board of Twentieth Century–Fox liked it, but *Planet of the Apes* was still not greenlighted. Fox had another daring science-fiction piece, *Fantastic Voyage*, and was keen to see if America was ready to take this genre to heart. It was. *Fantastic Voyage* was a smash success, and Zanuck finally agreed to proceed, provided that the budget should not exceed $5 million—half of what Jacobs had originally estimated. And of this sum, some 20 percent would be needed for makeup alone.

Planet of the Apes went into production in May 1967. Some of the locations in the Arizona desert were so far removed that the cast and crew had to be flown in by helicopter, and summer was hot as hell there. Fox was so worried that some other studio would steal the idea that the entire production was conducted in absolute secrecy. But it was worth it.

For me, the idea of a man thrust into this situation, with his companions gone, was the very essence of loneliness. Imagine, to be the only creature of your species left. I found it a very appealing part to play, but very hard physically. I was half-naked, most of the time, and got pelted with rocks, whipped, firehosed, caught in nets, and whatnot. I remember Joe Canutt, who doubled me in a lot of it, as in the scene where they catch me in a net and jerk me upside-down, coming up to me and saying ruefully, "You know Chuck, I remember when we used to win these things."

On June 19, Heston set a new precedent: for the first time in his career, he was stripped naked in front of the camera. He noted the experience in his journal: "Frank has thought of several telling touches to underline the dehumanizing of Taylor—stripping him in court, for one. It's the first time I've ever done a nude scene, even photographed from the rear."

Planet of the Apes opened in February 1968 to rave reviews and excellent box office. Perhaps *Newsweek*'s critic best expressed the film's underlying poignancy when he wrote that it "catches us at a particularly wretched moment in the course of human events, when we are perfectly willing to believe that man is despicable and a great deal lower than the lower animals." Pauline Kael, writing in the *New Yorker*,

had special praise for Heston, believing that "the movie could not have been so forceful or so funny with anyone else . He's an archetype of what makes Americans win . . . he represents American power. He is the perfect American Adam to work off some American guilt feelings or self-hatred on."

For all intents and purposes it looked to us like a film that could bring in a ton of money. It did, and it still does, I am happy to say. We just didn't anticipate that it would get good notices as well, and achieve the cult status that it has to this day.

Dick Zanuck, who had given the go-ahead for the film, was ecstatic. As Planet of the Apes soared at the box office, he gave me a call.

"Listen, we've really got to do a sequel."

"Ah, come on Dick," I replied. "We've told the story. If we do anything more it will just be further adventures among the monkeys."

"Chuck, I've got to do the sequel and I can't do it if you're not in it."

I gave this some thought. "Look, Dick," I said finally, "I'm very grateful to you for having green-lighted the film in the first place, so I'll do the sequel if you promise to kill me off in the first scene."

"Okay," I said. "Fair enough."

"And," I said, "you can pay me whatever you want and give the money to our school."

Both Fray and Zanuck's son went to the same

Opposite: As astronaut George Taylor in *Planet of the Apes*. Left: Facing James Whitmore at trial. Above: In chains with fellow human Linda Harrison.

school, and since I really wasn't interested in being involved with the sequel (or any sequel for that matter), this seemed to be an elegant way to return the favor and still stay at arm's length from the production. I didn't want to get involved in the sequel's script or in the casting; I just wanted to show up for the first scene and be done with it. Shortly before I was scheduled to start shooting, Dick Zanuck called again.

"Would it be okay," Zanuck asked, " if you disappeared in the first scene, and you got killed in the last?"

I gave it some thought.

"I guess. Okay, that's fair enough."

Today, thirty years after the release of the first picture, Fox is considering a remake of Planet of the Apes *(a project that may involve* Titanic *director James Cameron).*

MARC ANTONY IS ONE OF THE BEST PARTS *in Shakespeare, and possibly the easiest of parts. It probably has the single most powerful speech in all of Shakespeare, at least the beginning of which almost every schoolboy used to be able to quote: "Friends, Romans, countrymen, lend me your ears!" You never pass up a chance to waltz with the old gentleman.*

Of course, *Julius Caesar* and the role of Marc Antony has always had a special significance for Heston. He had played the part in the 16mm film production directed by David Bradley, which was for all intents and purposes his national film debut. He had returned to *Julius Caesar* again during the CBS "Studio One" days, and had joined Katharine Cornell in the Broadway production of *Antony and Cleopatra*. If there was one role in all of Shakespeare for which Chuck felt a special affinity, it was Marc Antony.

The proposal came from a young producer named Peter Snell. Snell originally had television in mind, but Commonwealth United figured that with Heston's name, the new production of *Julius Caesar* was feature material. Chuck agreed, providing he had his usual controls over the script and casting. He even agreed to keep his fee at the original $100,000 figure that he had previously agreed to for the television version—plus 15 percent of the world gross. Herman Citron, his agent, would have rolled his eyes, but The Iceman knew that when it came to Shakespeare, Heston couldn't be argued out of it.

With Heston on board, Snell was able to gather quite a formidable cast: Sir John Gielgud took the role of Caesar, Richard Johnson was cast as Cassius, and Richard Chamberlain would appear as Octavius. Orson Welles was approached for Brutus, and Welles seemed delighted. That left the role of Portia. In 1967, all of Britain (and the United States besides) was held in thrall by a very cool and sophisticated lady named Diana Rigg, who played the role of the visceral Emma Peel in the television series "The Avengers." Miss Rigg was schooled in Shakespeare, and it did not take much convincing to have her join the cast.

Before shooting started, Welles dropped out of the project, and Snell, with Heston's approval, approached Jason Robards, Jr. In addition to his film career, Robards was an accomplished stage actor who had won national recognition in the 1956 production of Eugene O'Neill's *The Iceman Cometh*. One year later he was awarded the New York Drama Critics Award for the same playwright's *Long Day's Journey Into Night*. Yet despite his verve with contemporary plays, Robards did not seem to have a knack for Shakespeare.

He was not good. I say this with some regret but it is true. Jason is a good enough actor to withstand criticism for one part. You have to understand, though, that it is a hard part; no, it is a terrible part. It is in many ways not unlike the role of Hamlet: that insecurity, the constant soul-searching over the moral justification of regicide. It's damn tough, and unfortunately, Jason didn't live up to it.

As Heston predicted, Robards's career survived the sometimes withering criticism of reviewers in Britain and the United States, and he later went on to win two Academy Awards.

John Gielgud shone as Julius Caesar, though.

Left: One more dance with the master. With John Gielgud as Caesar in *Julius Caesar*, 1970. Above: I stumbled through makeup and wardrobe in a sick daze and survived the morning, when fortunately, I only had to work behind the camera.

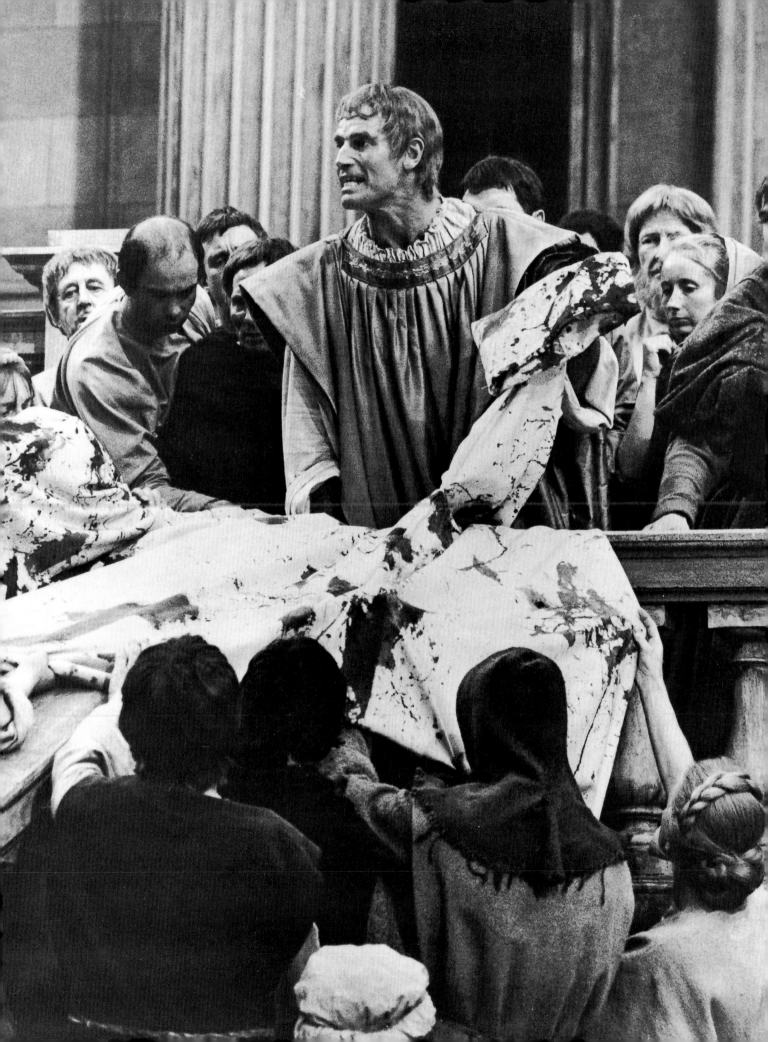

I never asked him, but I know for sure Gielgud has played Antony. And I'm sure he also played Brutus at one time or another—in fact, he played all the parts in the piece. I have one short scene with him, in the beginning. You know, Marc Antony is an odd part. Apart from the short scene with Caesar, he has only one other scene with any of the major characters, before the Battle of Philippi, that is. He sort of has it all to himself. So here we were doing the funeral oration, and Brutus comes up and gives a good speech, and then Shakespeare has Antony come up, and his speech is far superior. He says, "But Brutus is an honorable man! etc., etc." Well, anyway, we did the long shots and then we moved in for the close angles, in which Gielgud appeared as the bloody corpse of Caesar. That's the scene in which I pull the bloody toga off the bier and say, "Look you here,/Here is himself, marr'd, as you see, with traitors." So of course he had to be there in that shot, and sure enough, I pull the toga and there is Sir John as Caesar, acting quite dead. Afterwards I said, "John, it's been wonderful to play a scene with you again, even dead."

"Oh, well, I should stay offscreen to help you in your close-ups, Chuck," he said graciously, referring to the close-up angles in which the actor repeats his lines so that the editor can intersperse these with the master shots.

"No, no, that's sweet of you but don't do that, you're covered up anyway, an extra will do just fine."

"No, really, I should be glad to, I really would," John insisted.

I took a deep breath and looked him in the eye. "John, the last thing I need today is to do one of the great speeches in all of Shakespeare with one of the great actors of the century lying there, listening to me. Please, go home." He did.

BY THE TIME THE PRODUCTION WRAPPED, Heston and Snell were discussing the idea of making a sequel to *Julius Caesar*. The most obvious follow-up was *Antony and Cleopatra*, since Marc Antony figures in both plays. Shakespeare must have been especially intrigued with this character, since he is the only historical figure treated in depth in two separate Shakespeare plays. Their movie version of *Antony and Cleopatra* went into production three years later, appearing in release in 1973.

This was, to me, the most important film I've ever made. Antony and Cleopatra was the first play in which I appeared on Broadway, and it is just such a great play. I did the script for the film, the only script I've ever written. It may be that my redaction of the play for the screen version is the best thing I've ever written. But who would direct it?

I was trying to get either Laurence Olivier or Orson Welles to direct Antony and Cleopatra because to do Shakespeare on film, and do it well, you need a consummate film director with an in-depth knowledge of Shakespeare and the play. Well, the list of directors who can do all that is

As Caesar in *Antony and Cleopatra.*

painfully short. So I talked to both of them and interestingly enough, they came back with the same question.

"Do you have a great Cleopatra?"

"Well, great I don't know, you'll make her great."

"Can't do that. Cleopatra must *be great. That's one of the problems of the play,"* said Olivier.

Welles echoed his words: "If you don't find a great Cleopatra, you can't do this play, dear boy."

True words. It is the longest women's part in Shakespeare and perhaps the best woman's part in the world. She's all women—queen, lover, bitch, temptress, coward, heroine—all of these. Actresses who have played it usually reach three or four of those roles, but all of them—that's very rare, perhaps impossible.

Heston began to think that he had omitted one potential director from his list: himself. The evening before he was to shoot some

Left: *Antony and Cleopatra* is different. It not only takes place in Rome, Greece, Sicily, and Egypt, it is *about* those places. Above: Caesar on location.

screen tests in London, he had dinner with Frank Schaffner, who was busy preparing one of his best films, *Nicholas and Alexandra* (1971).

"I'm going to direct the tests myself," Chuck said, eyeing his friend.

"Oh, uh-huh."

"I actually may direct the film myself," Chuck continued, encouraged by the off-handed acceptance of his proposal, "depending on how things develop, you know."

"Sure," Frank said between mouthfuls. "Why not? Nothing to it."

The next day, there was one actress who came through very well in the tests—Hildegard Neil. She remembers it well: "Chuck had been looking for a Cleo for a long time. He had been in preparation for about a year and had obviously thought about lots of people, but at the time we met (in the winter of 1970) he was still very much in the searching stage. I was playing Helen of Troy at the Aldwych Theater, and I believe Chuck saw one of my performances."

Meanwhile, Snell had secured funding on the basis of pre-sales, as most independent films are produced and funded today. The production could proceed.

Left: No, I'm not angry here, just squinting through the lens. Above: I dragged that typewriter all over the world.

On the set, Chuck fell into the grueling routine of a director/actor: directing and acting during the day, preparing the next day's scene during the night. The loss of sleep grated on him, and ultimately had its effect. In his journal on July 22, in the sixth week of the ten-week schedule, he wrote: "I almost broke my career-long record of never having missed an hour of work time today. I woke with reasonable energy, but collapsed with giddiness while shaving, stomach churning. Lydia turned to and got me dressed and into the studio. I stumbled through makeup and wardrobe in a sick daze and survived the morning, when I fortunately only had to work behind the camera. Directors at least get to sit down. Having slept through the lunch break, I felt in better shape by the time I had to perform. I managed, I think, a good close-up for 'Where hast thou been, my heart. . . .'"

Looking back on the project, Chuck still remembers the acute challenge of being the writer, the director, and the actor, all at once. He believes that Neil's performance as Cleopatra may have suffered as a result: *Hildegard Neil was a good actress. It may have been my fault. I was also acting as Antony, and I may not have given her enough guidance.*

"He made her too soft," says Lydia, with a wink. "He likes his women to be soft, you see."

"Then how did I wind up marrying you?" Chuck retorts with feigned indignation.

BEFORE HESTON STEPPED IN FRONT of a camera again, he came to a critical crossroads in his life. After *Julius Caesar*, this group of prominent Democrats approached him to run for the U.S. Senate. And why not? Ronald Reagan, who had preceded Chuck as president of SAG, had moved on to the top spot in California, having successfully run for governor in 1966.

That query was not the first, and it wouldn't be the last, either. In just about every interview I give, the question is bound to come up: "Are you going to run for public office?" Well, I give them my standard answer, which is that I've already been president of the United States three times. But this time, they weren't kidding. The Democrats figured they could raise a war chest of several million to fund the campaign. So, they asked, "Will you do it?" I answered I would think about it. That's what I did, and talked it over with some of my friends who are in the know about this sort of thing. Interestingly enough, they all liked the idea and encouraged me to do it. Why? No reason other than that which has motivated men and women for centuries: just plain service to the nation.

When at long last I came back home from London, I broached the subject with my most important advisor, Lydia. She knows me better than anyone else, and was best qualified to render advice. So my girl heard me out, thought about it, and then asked a simple question: "But what do you want, Charlie?" It was as if the light went on.

Suddenly, I realized that deep down inside, I didn't want to do it. The thought of never being able to act again, go on stage, or wait for the first take was simply unbearable. The next day, I called them up and said, "Thanks, but no thanks."

SOYLENT GREEN was set in a world when the population of New York is forty-eight million people. In a sense it is really about the population explosion. It was also one of those films that, in an awkward phrase, I "caused to be made." It turned into a good film, as much as anything else because of Eddie Robinson's performance, which was simply wonderful.

    Soylent Green (1973) was produced by Walter Seltzer in collaboration with Russell Thatcher, who had turned to Richard Fleischer to direct. Their choice of Fleischer was sound: the director was responsible for *Fantastic Voyage*, which, together with *Planet of the Apes*, can be credited with having launched science fiction as a mature Hollywood genre. Before that, Walt Disney had picked him to direct one of the first Disney live-action features, 20,000 *Leagues Under the Sea.*

    Soylent Green depicts a world in which population growth has far outpaced society's ability to provide food and essential services. People overwhelm the city like vermin; they live in packed apartments, in stairwells, on

Left: The little wine and cheese farewell where we lifted a glass to Eddie Robinson, not knowing that he would be dead in days. Above: With the cast of *Soylent Green*.

rooftops, in sewers, on the streets. High above these lowly creatures lives a caste of fabulously wealthy industrialists and politicians, who can still afford the impossible luxury of food and a private apartment. It is in one of these dwellings that a murder is committed, which a police detective by the name of Thorn (played by Heston) is ordered to investigate.

Thorn lives much like the rest of New York: he shares a grubby apartment with Sol Roth (Edward G. Robinson) and tries to survive on a sickly green bar of synthetic nutrition, which its manufacturer has christened "Soylent Green." No one quite knows what this substance is made of, but people fight for it anyway—except Sol, who can still vividly remember wondrous things like steak and salad.

The film, which was based on the Harry Harrison novel *Make Room! Make Room!*, is cynical about society and its capacity to cope with modern ills, and has an added sense of urgency—perhaps because the danger of overpopulation had first come to public attention in the 1970s. Still, critics took a while to warm to the film. The initial reviews were mixed, but today *Soylent Green* is considered one of Heston's finest movies and a bona fide cult film that enjoys repeat performances at film festivals and art theaters. Perhaps a key to its success is the screen chemistry between Heston and Robinson.

I believe it is one of my best performances too, and I have often wondered if it was because of some subliminal communication between us, about what he was going through. You see, it was Eddie's last movie. He knew he was dying when he shot it, but he didn't tell anybody. Now there is this scene in which he dies, and as production schedules go, scenes are shot at random, depending on the location, the set, and the scheduling of the actors. But by an odd stroke of fate, this was really the last scene that Eddie was supposed to do. He was wonderful in the scene, taking the poison that will kill him, then lying back on the gurney waiting for death to come, while above him a giant film screen shows him, one last time, all the wonderful things of a world long gone: mountains, streams, wildlife, flowers. Afterwards, we had a little party with wine and cheese, as is often the case when a leading actor is done with a picture, and ten days later he was dead.

Just imagine what it would have been like for him to lie there in that scene, pretending to be dying, and knowing that it will be the last take he would ever do. Never go over a script again. Never go on stage again. He is so good in it, and in hindsight it is not difficult to imagine why.

AFTER THE CYNICAL, angst-ridden *Soylent Green*, *The Three Musketeers* (1973) is a dramatically different movie—a film that breathes a refreshing air of comedy and irreverence so rare in the disenchanted years of the early 1970s. Few directors would have risen to the occasion as ably as Richard Lester, a director who with *A Hard Day's Night* (1964) and *Help!* (1965), both starring the Beatles, made zany humor a British cinematic tradition well before the *Monty Python* days.

Lester called me up, after he had sent me the script. It was a very good script, written by George MacDonald Fraser—one of the very few scripts that I've read of which you say, go ahead, shoot it, it's fine the way it is. Khartoum was such a script. This was another one.

He wanted me to play one of the musketeers. I thought, Oh no, here we go again, they're going to be sloshing around in Spain in winter, doing sword fights and horse falls, and I thought, No . . . Not now. So I called Dick back, and told him, "Look, it's a wonderful script, but I really don't think I should."

"Why not?" Lester asked.

"Well, you guys are going to be hacking away all winter. But, I tell you, the script is really great. Come to think of it, couldn't I play a cameo role, like the Duke of Buckingham or something, a nice short part?

"I've got a better idea," Lester replied. "Why don't you do Cardinal Richelieu?"

"Oh, I don't know if I can play that."

"Yes, you can," was his determined reply. "Sure you can." So I did, even though it was kind of a stretch, and I admit I enjoyed it very much. Also, it is the one role in which I got to have a bigger nose than my real one. A wonderful false nose and all kinds of good stuff.

"Actors love that kind of thing," Lydia says knowingly.

The film, inspired by the novel of Alexandre Dumas, tells the story of a young man of humble upbringing named d'Artagnan (played by Michael York) who travels to the court of Louis XIV in Paris in hopes of become the king's musketeer. He is challenged to a duel by three veteran musketeers, who take the tempestuous youth under their wing. Before long, they become embroiled in a plot, spun by the sinister Cardinal Richelieu, to increase his already considerable power over the king. The Cardinal plans to expose an affair between the king's consort, Anne (Geraldine Chaplin), and the British Duke of Buckingham (Simon Ward). He enlists the shrewd Milady de Winter (Faye Dunaway) to help him. Of course, it is up to the musketeers to thwart the plot and to save the Queen's honor.

As he has always done with the characters he plays, Heston thoroughly investigated the history of the cardinal who held such great power over France in the early years of Louis XIV.

There was a line that I ran across in one of the biographies of Richelieu that impressed me so much, I got Richard to put it in the script. Someone said to Richelieu, "Your Eminence, it must be dreadful to have so many enemies." The cardinal replied,

"I? I have no enemies. France has enemies." Or, as Louis XIV would later say, "Messieurs, l'État, c'est Moi."

The Three Musketeers is delicious entertainment, not in the least because Lester, always the social historian, used Dumas's wit to expose the awful class differences in pre-Revolutionary France. When d'Artagnan and his servant Planchet, bound for England, try to talk their way past the French border guards with a stolen *passe-partout* (or "passport"), the official retorts that the pass is good for only one person. "And correctly so," says d'Artagnan hautily, "I am only one. That there," he says, pointing to Planchet, "is a *servant.*"

The stellar cast was clearly having a good time with the splendid costumes, the impressive sets, and the swashbuckling, bloodless duels, and it shows in the finished picture. Heston is a devilishly duplicitous figure with his pointy Vandyke beard, feigning a suave gentility while plotting the death of the king's men and the downfall of France's queen. He enjoyed working with his co-stars, including Faye Dunaway and Raquel Welch. "It was a brilliant stroke of Dick's," he says, "to make Raquel, as beautiful as she was, very clumsy. She kept falling and stumbling over stuff. She put the key down in her bosom and then she couldn't get the key out—wonderfully funny."

However, Lester had quite a surprise in store for his actors and actresses. "I had a feeling that something was afoot," Faye Dunaway wrote in her recent autobiography. Having screened the film, Dunaway was shocked to see a trailer announcing, for all intents and purposes, a sequel. Lester had decided to split the finished material into two separate releases: *The Three Musketeers* in 1974, and *The Four Musketeers: Milady's Revenge* in 1975. "There was an immediate outcry from the actors that we had been taken advantage of," Dunaway wrote. "No one had agreed to the idea of filming two movies for the price of one."

I was paid a very great deal of money for not much work, since my schedule was limited to ten days on the set. I thought it was kind of funny, but then again I didn't work so hard in it.

The Three Musketeers was a smash hit, both with the critics and the public. The picture was nominated for the Golden Globe as Best Motion Picture-Musical/Comedy, and Raquel Welch won the Golden Globe as Best Actress.

Heston has a large portrait of himself as Cardinal Richelieu hanging in the corridor outside the screening room in his home. He explains where it came from:

Well, in 1989, they were doing a sequel, called The Return of the Musketeers. *Lester called, and I thought he was going to offer me a part in it. But when I asked him, he said, "No no, I can't do that."*

"You son of a bitch," I said, "you've got everyone else in this one."

"That's true," Lester admitted, "but you're dead. It's twenty years later, and there's a different cardinal now—you know, whatshisname, Mazarin."

I was dumbfounded.

"But we would like your permission," Lester continued, "to have a portrait made of you—you know, to have hanging on the wall and show the continuity."

So I said, "The hell with you guys."

"Oh, come on, Chuck," Lester said suavely.

"All right then," I said, "I'll do it if you give me the portrait after you're done with it."

Now, mind you, I thought this was going to be a small portrait, you know, fairly modest. But in due course it came over and there it was, some five feet tall. It's a good portrait. I'm very fond of it. It's painted very much in the style of the period.

Left: This is one of Dick Lester's best ideas in *The Three Musketeers*. A grand ball is staged, and all the guests, including Faye as Milady de Winter, are dressed in gleaming white. Only the Cardinal retains his crimson robes. Above: As Cardinal Richelieu in *The Three Musketeers*. It was the one role in which I've got a bigger nose than the one I usually have.

The New

You get a dozen or so disparate people together and put them in a dangerous situation. Voilà: you've got yourself a disaster epic.

HOLLYWOOD

AS THE 1970s PROGRESSED, Heston career continued unabated, but at a slower pace. The years of "riding the tiger," of jetting from one location to the next, were past. The country's recession was taking a stiff toll on the movie business. The time had come for him to pick his parts carefully from the diminishing roster of films that Hollywood was putting in production.

Meanwhile, the nation was living through an additional trauma—that of Watergate. In the summer of 1974, Richard Nixon announced that he was resigning the office of the presidency. Heston had met Nixon and liked his concern for the state of the arts in America. The feeling coincided with Heston's disenchantment with the Democrats and particularly, the Democratic nominee in the 1972 elections, George McGovern. He and Lydia attended Nixon's second inauguration. From then on he jetted often to Washington, D.C., either on behalf of the National Council on the Arts, the American Film Institute, or for SAG, whose board he still assists from time to time.

In 1973, Heston was planning an AFI Life Achievement Award ceremony for the great director John Ford when, to his surprise, Nixon indicated his desire to attend. So, at the event on March 31, Heston stood up to introduce the thirty-seventh president of the United States—"a job," he later confessed in his journal, "which tends to hold your attention." Nixon presented Ford with the Medal of Freedom. "It's valuable to the industry as a whole," Heston commented, "since it'll be the first time any U.S. president has involved himself in anything in film . . . even attending a premiere." U.S. presidents have done it ever since, including Bill Clinton, who in December 1997 bestowed the Kennedy Center Honor Award on a visibly moved Charlton Heston during a telecast ceremony.

The film industry was going through one of its worst doldrums, with weekly attendance dropping from 38 million in 1966 to as low as 15.8 million in 1971. In 1971, Columbia reported an astounding $28 million loss. Of course, studio executives were quick to point to the nation's economy as the reason. The country was in a recession. Inflation had hit the 10 percent mark and beyond. Unemployment soared to 7 percent. Housing starts were down 40 percent. There were long lines in front of the gas

About to die (yet again), trying to save my bitchy wife in *Earthquake*. George Kennedy is at right. He survives.

pumps after the Gulf States decided to cut off the oil supply to the West as punishment for their support of Israel during the October War of 1973.

Beset by financial problems, the studios became a target for takeovers. In 1969, Las Vegas hotel magnate Kirk Kerkorian took control of one of Hollywood's oldest studios, MGM. In May 1970, the once venerable institution that had funded *Ben-Hur* was reduced to auctioning most of its props and costumes. One year later, MGM briefly flirted with the idea of merging with Twentieth Century–Fox, but never went through with it.

The studios needed a break, and they got one in 1971 when Nixon granted Hollywood a 7 percent tax credit on domestic films. The idea was to encourage studios to reinvest the savings in new productions at home, rather than abroad. Heston had lobbied hard for the tax credit, but it was not until Governor Reagan had made a personal appeal that Nixon consented to the measure. Still, Hollywood productions had slowed to a trickle.

By 1973, though, the studios saw their situation begin to improve. Just as theatergoers had flocked to historical epics in the days of early television, audiences now embraced a new genre that somehow connected with the apocalyptic feel of the times: disaster movies. In 1973, *The Poseidon Adventure* earned an astounding $40 million for its studio, more than double the amount of its leading competitor, *Deliverance*.

THE DISASTER PICTURES WERE *a phenomenon that lasted several years. Basically, the picture works like this: You get a dozen or so disparate people that have no obvious connection to one another, and put them collectively in a dangerous situation. Of course, by this time the technology had advanced to a point where the actual disasters could be filmed with quite convincing special effects, like the* Towering Inferno *and in my case,* Earthquake. *The thing is, to make this formula work, you need well-known actors to fill the principal roles. You see, there is not enough time to flesh out all of these characters, so that each of the future victims only get a short introduction. If the actor or actress in question is readily recognizable, people will say, "Oh look, that's so-and-so," and they'll remember the role he or she is supposed to play. You don't* want *people to turn to each other midway in the movie and say, "I thought the fire chief was Paul Newman. . . ."*

Now, you must understand, none of the films were creatively very good. At best, they were technologically impressive, and as we knew beforehand, hugely successful. And all of us—Steve McQueen, Paul Newman, Burt Lancaster, myself—we at least did one or two, because that's what the public wanted. Besides, you didn't have to work much; each of us did maybe two or three weeks of shooting, the rest was special effects, and you walked away with a lot of money, particularly those of us who were paid a piece of the first-dollar gross.

In Earthquake, *I play this marvelously gifted architect who has known all along that Los Angeles is in danger of a major earthquake, and has a plan to solve it. So I read through the script and I came upon the ending, which didn't impress me. Mind you, I had script approval, so I went back to the studio and said, "Look, guys. Why not do something different? Surprise 'em. Why don't we have him try to rescue his wife and he drowns too?"*

The Universal people hated the idea. "Oh, no, Chuck, no way," they said. "Are you kiddin'? We need you to survive and rebuild Los Angeles."

"Surprise 'em. I think the audience is ready for an ending like that."

"No, Chuck. We can't do that."

I had script approval, so in the end, they grudgingly agreed. It's amazing when you think of it. People always assume the hero has to live. That's not true. Take me, for example. I have died at least a dozen times. Perhaps, in my case, they have gotten used to it. Or maybe they look forward to it, I don't know.

"You must understand," says Lydia, "he *loves* death scenes."

In order to give audiences the actual feel of the earth rumbling under their feet, Universal developed a new sound system that added very low-frequency noise to the soundtrack. When played back through low-pitch woofers, the noise produced air vibrations in the theater which viewers, immersed in the sounds and sights of a major earthquake, readily accepted as earth tremors.

It was called Sensurround, and let me tell you, it really "sensed around!" You got the vibrations. I was there, in Grauman's Chinese Theater, when the film opened. During the earthquake scene, I looked up and saw some of the plaster fall from the ceiling. You can't ask for more realism.

The Academy seemed to agree. *Earthquake* won two Oscars: one for Sound, and a Special Achievement Award for Visual Effects.

FOR UNIVERSAL, DISASTER MOVIES were becoming a sort of house specialty of the 1970s. Given the extraordinary success in 1970 of *Airport*, based on the novel by Arthur Hailey, they decided to do a remake and turned to Heston to take the lead role. Of course, by then the plane was no longer a Boeing 707 but a 747 jumbo jet (which entered commercial service in 1972). In *Airport 1975* (1974), one of these "heavies" collides with a private plane in a storm, killing one pilot and injuring the other. In desperation, the stewardess takes the controls and flies the 747 until an Air Force plane comes to the rescue by lowering a pilot through the hole in the cockpit.

As a pilot in *Airport 1975*. The new Hollywood consisted largely of disaster films, of which I did my share.

I went down to Dallas to learn to fly. Believe it or not, I flew the 747. It's a very easy aircraft to fly. They took me to this simulator which is very real—so real, in fact, that when you crash, you know it. Today you'd call the 747 a very user-friendly aircraft. I'm convinced I could have taken one off. I would not have wanted to land one, but all you do is wait till the gauges reach the proper setting, you rotate, and it will take off!

THE NEXT ALL-STAR JEOPARDY MOVIE was not so much a disaster movie as an old-fashioned war epic. The year was 1976. The Bicentennial mood was in the air, a new president was in the White House, and Universal felt that the time had come for a feel-good, patriotic war picture. It turned to producer Walter Mirisch to reenact the Battle of Midway—the turning point of the war in the Pacific during World War II.

The film was called *Midway*. Heston played Captain Matt Garth.

Wonderful actors played in it, and I enjoyed performing with them. Early on, we had several breakfast meetings at the Polo Lounge to talk about the movie and shaping the characters. It was then that we arrived at the idea of me playing a fictional character, while all the others would play actual officers who figured prominently in the battle. At one

Above: Flying a 747 is surprisingly simple. It's what you would call a very user-friendly aircraft. Right: With Gloria Swanson on the set of *Airport 1975*. Hers is actually one of the most interesting performances in the film.

With the cast of *Midway* on the Lexington. Walter Mirisch, the producer, said, "If we get Hank Fonda to play Nimitz, we'll get anyone we want." He was right.

point, Walter said, "If I can get Hank Fonda to play Nimitz, which isn't a very large role, then we'll get anyone we want." All the actors playing those parts really got a ridiculously low sum, like ten or fifteen thousand dollars, so whoever came in really did it as a labor of love. Except me, I have to admit, because I got my piece of the gross. Anyway, I told Walter I didn't think Hank would do that part for that small a fee. I was wrong. What I forgot was that Hank had been in the Navy. He was in the Pacific on Nimitz's staff. He was an admirer of Nimitz, and so with Hank we did get anyone we wanted.

The picture could not have been made except for two circumstances, over which no one had any control. One was the fact that we needed a World War II–class carrier. There was only one such ship still in existence. It was the Lexington, which the Navy was using to qualify pilots on carrier landings and takeoffs. The Navy was very gracious and allowed us to shoot exteriors on the Lexington. The other thing that we absolutely *needed was color combat footage. Of all the combatants on both sides in World War II, the only ones to use color film were the U.S. Navy and the Japanese Navy. And so we got the footage we needed—from both the Japanese and the American side.*

Working with Henry Fonda was something very special for Heston, who has always harbored a deep admiration for the actor. In his journal, he wrote about the experience.

He looks marvelous at seventy. I had a short scene to play with him, my contribution consisting entirely of "Aye, aye, sir." Nevertheless, I was impressed to be in a shot with him, recalling things I've liked all the way back to Drums Along the Mohawk *(1939). He looks amazingly like Nimitz and is very good in the role, too, not surprisingly.*

"It was a very successful movie, in no small part due to Walter Mirisch, who was a wonderful producer," Lydia says. "To this day, the Mirisches are among our closest friends."

Not all of Heston's film choices during this period were right on the money. In July 1975, Fox offered him the lead role in a picture called *The Antichrist*. Perhaps the title put him off, or perhaps it was the subject—a quasi-horror story in the tradition of *Rosemary's Baby*. "You have to be skeptical of accepting an offer just to reassure yourself that you're employable," he wrote. "This Fox film could have been effective, if perfectly done, but it could have come off very cheaply, too. On top of which, it would've put me overseas throughout the fall." He declined. Gregory Peck took the role instead. The film was renamed *The Omen* and it became the smash hit of 1976.

THEY ARE MARVELOUS BOATS, *these big submarines. You cannot help but be impressed by the size.*

Once again, Heston's excellent credentials in Washington had paid off. He had gone to sea on one of the Navy's new nuclear submarines to see what life was like deep under the ocean—and to take notes for his new action/adventure feature, *Gray Lady Down* (1978).

The director of the picture, David Greene, was British and therefore not allowed to come on board an American nuclear submarine. I was the only representative on the project who actually sailed on a "boomer." Actually, it's quite commodious. You have no sense of motion—it feels like you are in a normal room, stateside.

You see, we were doing this practice exercise, while the surface fleet was trying to sink us.

"What!?" Lydia says, realizing that these details were withheld from her at the time. "And you weren't afraid? You didn't feel any type of claustrophobia?"

Not at all. I'm sure that it's different aboard a diesel sub; I've never sailed on one of those. But nuclear boats—they call them boats, *whereas everything else that floats in the Navy is called a* ship—*are quite large and quite comfortable. I spent two days at sea, and I felt right at home.*

Joining Navy sailors on a real mission on the high seas gave Heston some interesting insights, which he later put to good use.

Did you know, for example, that the submarine service is the only branch where the officers can grow beards? I thought that would be an interesting idea. I've worn false and real beards in many films, but I thought that growing a natural beard for this picture would be a nice touch. The director agreed.

"I could have done without it," Lydia remarks dryly.

Gray Lady Down, also produced by Walter Mirisch, was based on the David Lavallee novel *Event 1000,* in which a submarine captain, Captain Blanchard (played by Heston), is about to return his boat to Norfolk and himself

Left and above: *Grey Lady Down* was an early precursor of the nuclear submarine action films. One interesting detail I learned was that submariners are the only officers in the U.S. Navy allowed to wear a beard. I made good use of the opportunity.

to a new position behind a desk. While the officers celebrate the changing of command, the submarine hits a freighter in dense fog and sinks to the bottom. It is only with the aid of a new submersible rescue craft that the crew is ultimately retrieved from the wreck, but the officer in charge of the rescue effort, Captain Gates (played by David Carradine) is killed in the process.

Originally the plot allowed for a Soviet submarine to be searching for us—not with the intent to help in the rescue, but to sink us. The studio bosses at Universal, however, thought that over and felt that, in the wake of détente and the SALT arms-limitation agreement, this would be counterproductive. They struck that part from the script. Of course, a few years later, when we were back to calling the Soviet Union the "evil empire," it would most likely have remained in the picture.

Gray Lady Down was released in 1977 and did rather well at the box office.

A fur trapper in *Wind River/The Mountain Men*.

IN JUNE 1974, FRASER HESTON was nineteen years old. He had switched from studying marine biology at UCSD to literature at UCLA. An avid outdoorsman, he was earning his keep that summer in Colorado as an apprentice river-rafting tour guide. The Colorado River was unusually high that summer, and in one of the rapids Fray's raft flipped over, trapping the passengers. Fray fought himself clear of the foaming water and, with the help of an army convoy, saved all but two of the tourists, who drowned. The incident made a deep impression on him and perhaps added a new sense of awe and respect to his deep love of nature.

When Fraser decided to become a screenwriter, it didn't surprise his family that he was drawn most to themes of the great outdoors in which man struggles to make an existence. One such script, his first that made it to the screen (in 1980), was called *Wind River*.

It tells the story of fur trappers in the American West in the 1830s. A producer, Martin Ransohoff, picked it up and showed it to Columbia. The studio bought it and put the picture in production. Ransohoff offered me the lead; I was delighted to accept and perform in a film written by my son—and what father wouldn't have?

Wind River's character, Bill Tyler, is a very compelling role. It is a part I've played on stage and on film several times before—the type of man who realizes that he's had a great run, but that his time is coming to an end. Tyler had struck gold when beaver hats were in fashion and beaver pelts were in great demand, but now, fashion had changed in favor of silk hats. The market had disappeared, bringing huge losses to the big fur-trading companies. But Tyler is a loner. He goes out with his partner named Frapp (Brian Keith) and figures that for one last time, they can bring in enough to see them through.

Fraser's script had, shall we say, an elegiac quality. That is very hard to capture on film, but I think we succeeded by shooting on wonderful, truly monumental locations like Yellowstone and the Rockies. Our disappointment came when, during postproduction, much of that wonderfully inspiring footage was cut and the editors focused on exploiting the raw action between Frapp and Tyler. It violated the agreement I thought we had with Ransohoff about what the picture should be about. Prior to the release they changed the title to The Mountain Men, *which is how it went into the theaters. It did not fare very well. The sad thing is, this could have been a great film for both Fray and myself.*

But the decade ended on a high note. During the Oscar ceremonies in 1978, Heston was once again invited to the stage, this time to receive the Jean Hersholt Humanitarian Award. It was a moment to look back on a rich and rewarding career as one of Hollywood's most enduring stars. But Heston had no intention of resting on his laurels. Outside the auditorium, the world of entertainment was changing once again. And he was determined to be a part of it.

Receiving the Jean Hersholt Humanitarian Award from Bette Davis in 1978 during the 50th Annual Academy Awards—a great honor for which I am deeply grateful.

Hollywood's Eld

"Would have made milch the burning eyes of heaven, And passion in the gods."

er STATESMAN

PETER FALK, A K A INSPECTOR
Columbo, sizes up his suspect. "What's that?" he asks, pointing to a bulky device with silver-plated knobs. "That," says the man, "is a videocassette recorder." "Is that so?" says Columbo with sudden interest.

For many Americans, this 1976 episode with America's most beloved sleuth was their first encounter with the new technology. Most people didn't grasp its function or its significance. "A passing fad for techno-enthusiasts," was the prediction in the *New York Times*. After all, for thirty-five years since World War II, people had watched movies in one of two ways: on network television, or in a theater. That was all there was to it, and people were quite content.

Then came the 1980s and the world was suddenly inundated with media technology. First came Sony's Betamax video-recorder system, followed by a device called Laservision, which used a laser to read video images from a disc. At the same time, television itself was being revolutionized by the development of cable networks.

All these inventions affected Hollywood. Once the studios acknowledged that video was not a threat to their business but a new market for exploitation, they stopped licensing their features to video distributors and began to manufacture videos and laser discs themselves. In addition, the plethora of new media allowed the studios to go back and release older movies, including Heston's, on cable television, videocassette, and laser disc, thus introducing the actor's work to a new generation of viewers. Today, video has grown to be the third most important market for Hollywood films, after domestic and international theatrical release. In fact, many new movies and children's films are never shown in theaters, but are instead released "direct to video."

Heston embraced the multimedia age with open arms. In the years that followed, he starred in Hollywood films as well as cable television and network specials; he returned to the stage for some of his most memorable performances; and he created a documentary on the Bible that spawned a television series, a CD soundtrack, and a set of CD-ROMs. At a time when most actors and actresses of his generation were beginning to fade from the scene, it seemed that Heston's career had just been reinvented.

You look to the film work to increase your net worth and maintain your public identity, keeping your eye open for the now-and-then very good film. The stage, well, that's to keep your muscles stretched and, once in a while, take a shot at the real man-killers . . . And, as it turned out, I think I did a good deal of my best work through this period of time on stage and elsewhere. In the meantime, I was kept busy with lots of other things as well.

Shortly after his inauguration, President Reagan asked Heston to serve his country once again and co-chair a Presidential Task Force on the National Endowment for the Arts and Humanities. Many Republicans believed then, as they do now, that the NEA and NEH were outdated vehicles of federal largesse in an age when good art and music should sustain itself with corporate sponsorship and loyal patronage. The new president was under pressure to demonstrate that, despite his former career as an actor, he could rule objectively and decisively on this issue.

Heston turned to a number of friends and colleagues, including Frank Schaffner, Bob Fryer, Roger Stevens, Beverly Sills, and Franklin Roche, to help him sort through the vast range of NEA projects. Together with his co-chair, University of Chicago's Hanna Gray, Chuck established a base in Washington, D.C., for his Task Force and flew throughout the country to see NEA and NEH projects firsthand.

Our mandate was simple. We were to determine what the endowments did, how well they did it, and whether it was worth our tax money. It was kind of interesting. The idea was whether those two bodies were doing useful work. Now, mind you, it was widely presumed that I was doing a hatchet job. I was to dismantle at least the Endowment for the Arts which, if truth be told, at the time had gotten itself involved with some crappy things that were played up big in the press.

The response from the arts community was overwhelming. In the July 1981 issue

of *American Arts*, Heston asserted that "the White House was originally a little surprised at the level, the *volume*, of response in the arts community and how clearly
audible it was. After all, vastly more important sections of the economy feel the same
anxiety at having their slice of the pie diminished, but have not been heard as clearly."
I told them, "You have to recognize that people in the arts are highly visible, usually
fairly effective communicators. You're going to hear from them." And hear from
them he did. As Heston later said, "Many of these groups had determined before our
first session that the President had convened a new Spanish Inquisition and I was the
Lord High Executioner. I spent almost as much time doing interviews denying this
as I did chairing meetings."

Perhaps to the surprise of some Republicans in Washington, Heston came back
to the capital with the finding that the government *did* have a role in supporting the
arts and the humanities—but that, at the same time, the government should keep a
close watch on how the money was spent, as it should on any other executive branch.

*And then we did an amazing thing. We spent months traveling and meeting and
writing reports, and we came to the conclusion that, by and large, these institutions
were useful. And then we dismantled the Task Force. With all of our impressive offices
and letterheads and secretaries, we simply called it quits and went home—much to the
dismay to some members of the press. It was perhaps my greatest achievement in Washington. Sure, we could have continued as long as we wanted as some sort of advisory
body, but we said, "Okay, it's over. No point in spending any more taxpayers' money."*

Heston is too modest to say it, but it is much to his credit that the NEA was
saved from the ax of Reaganomics.

Public service, however, was not without its trials. Most people know Ed Asner
as the pudgy and sometimes cantankerous character from *The Mary Tyler Moore
Show* and *Lou Grant*, for which he won four Emmy Awards. But Asner, an outspoken
liberal, had also become the new president of the Screen Actors Guild. Asner felt he
should use this body to raise funds for Marxist guerrillas in Salvador, in Central
America. Heston took Asner head-on, not only because he felt that Reagan's war on
Communist agitation in Central America was justified but, more importantly because as SAG's former president he was concerned that the Guild should focus on
the problems for which it had been created. Heston was old enough to remember the
deep rifts created by the HUAC hearings, and he was convinced that politics had no
place in a union which collected dues from actors for the sole purpose of furthering
their interests. What's more, SAG had enough on its plate in view of the growing
unemployment of Hollywood actors in the early 1980s.

Heston feared that Asner's advocacy would do nothing but polarize Hollywood
into left and right all over again, and it nearly did when the AFL-CIO, always in search

Chairing the AFI, with Roger Stevens (far left), George Stevens (second from right), Gregory Peck (far right), and others.

of good publicity, hastened to Asner's side. Months of protests and ugly name-calling ensued. The animosity between the two camps was heightened when Asner proposed to merge SAG with the guild representing screen extras. The high cost of shooting in Los Angeles had driven many producers to shoot in non-union cities in California and Canada, and SAG believed that the combined memberships would wield greater leverage to curb the use of non-union labor. Heston (and a large group of SAG members besides) argued that while the problem was real, the proposed solution was flawed, since the two professions were very different, and should not be merged under one roof. In the heated debates that followed, Asner was overheard saying that actors like Heston had a "master-race" mentality.

Shortly thereafter, in March 1984, Chuck received a death threat from an obscure group called the "Workers Death Squad." Heston blamed the threat on the rhetoric espoused by the SAG leadership. In the years to come, Chuck remained a vocal opponent of many of SAG's policies which he felt undermined the very principles that SAG was supposed to uphold.

I WAS ONE OF THE PEOPLE who got a call from the Stanford Research Institute. They were investigating whether there should be an American Film Institute, and if so, what it should do. I said I thought it was a good idea. I was an advisor to the Council on the Arts but when my term ran out, they asked me to join the board of the American Film Institute. I did. You know, when they come knocking and ask you to do something like this, you're supposed to do it. That's been a very odd thing from the beginning of my career. It got me involved with the Screen Actors Guild—taking on the job of SAG president, which Reagan wanted me to accept after he resigned—followed by the NEA, the American Film Institute, and many others. These things keep coming up. They say, "Chuck you have to do this," and I say, "Oh, all right, if you think so."

Lydia, laughs, shaking her head. "You weren't exactly ducking, either, darling."

Well, now, I sure as hell never applied for these jobs.

"True," Lydia says, a smile on her lips.

Politics/public service has been a fixture of my career all along, and if I have contributed something that helped people in the process, for that I'm grateful. And so it happened with the AFI. I was just a member on the board, and at one point excused myself to go to the bathroom. I came back, and what do you know, they had made me chairman in my absence. The morale of the story is: never get up to go to the bathroom during a meeting! But I was, and continue to be, proud of the work of the American Film Institute.

FRASER HESTON, WHO IN 1980 married a young Canadian girl named Marilyn Pernfuss, had settled in Canada and written a new screenplay. *Mother Lode* (1982) describes the adventures of a young couple, Jean Dupré and Andrea Spalding, who enter the wilderness of British Columbia looking for a friend—a prospector in search of a "mother lode" of gold deposits. During their trek they come across an old Indian, a half-crazy Scotsman, and the Scotsman's twin brother, who ultimately leads them to an abandoned mine, where the couple is nearly killed. It was a classic Fraser Heston script, with an emphasis on magnificent scenery and outdoor adventure. Not surprisingly, *Mother Lode* became a family enterprise. Chuck took on the role of the villain, the crazy Scotsman (and his double, of course); Fraser doubled too, as writer and producer; Lydia shot the production stills; and Fraser's wife, Marilyn, served as the publicist. Most important, Chuck accepted the responsibility of directing the feature—the second time he directed a film since *Antony and Cleopatra*. Fraser's production company, Agamemnon Films, became the production company on record.

There was this actress who had had a small part in a previous picture, but who was still largely unknown. Her name was Kim Basinger. You could say I discovered her—a small claim to fame.

Kim was very good in the film. She was cast as Andrea, and Nick Mancuso as Jean. The only drawback was that she and Nick just hated each other on the set. Unfortunately, they are supposed to be young starry-eyed lovers in the film. I exercised my best diplomacy to get them through the scenes without actually having them bite each other's noses off. I barely succeeded. There was this scene where she sees me as the villain's twin brother, and runs away, terrified, into the arms of her lover, who then is supposed to comfort her. She simply couldn't stand doing that scene, to be embraced by this terrible man. I cleared the set—the only time I have ever done that as a director—and threw everybody else out. Then I turned to her and I said, "Kim, you have to do this scene. They call it acting. You have to allow Nick to embrace you and be grateful for it." She took a breath and did it. From then on, she was all right, and the movie set her off on her path to stardom.

I like directing on film. You see, there is a difference. In film, the director is really the prime creator. On stage, you direct the actors, and in the end you have to surrender to them. In film, the director ultimately makes the movie. He's the one who's up at three o'clock in the morning and runs through his mind the footage he's going to shoot that day. It's all in there, and he is responsible for committing it to celluloid.

Opposite: As the half-crazy Scotsman McGee in *Mother Lode,* 1982, a family project of sorts. Left: With Fraser and Kim Basinger on the set. Above: Fray wrote the script and co-produced *Mother Lode* in 1982.

"It's the *auteur* theory of directing that, I think, Chuck is most comfortable with," Lydia says. "Film is a *director's* medium."

True. My problem is that I don't like the idea of directing a film in which I don't have an acting role. Acting is really what I do—it's my life. To spend over a year or two in preproduction, production, and editing without acting, without ever taking a part in it, is very difficult for me. Perhaps that's why I haven't directed more films, even though I enjoy doing it.

Still, in the years to come, Heston would sit in the director's chair more often than he ever had before.

CHUCK HAD HIS EYES on television once more. In 1981, he joined the reigning prime-time series "Dynasty" in the role of Jason Colby. Some people wondered why an actor of Heston's stature would want to appear in a prime-time soap, no matter how popular. They missed the point. As he has often said, "Doing rather less challenging parts in huge commercial successes gives me the freedom to do things I love—play the real giants on the stage." The proceeds from TV work such as "Chiefs" (1983) and "The Colbys" (1985) made it possible for Chuck to pursue plays such as *Caine Mutiny*,

Left: With the cast of "The Colbys" in 1985. Above: As Sir Thomas More with his wife, played by Vanessa Redgrave, in the 1988 production of *A Man for All Seasons*, one of the first films made for Ted Turner's cable network.

The Crucifer of Blood, Detective Story, and A Man for All Seasons. (The latter was a successful British production in which Chuck starred as Sir Thomas More for a six-month run.)

During this time, some three thousand miles away, cable entrepreneur Ted Turner was getting ready to launch a new all-movies network to compete with Time/Warner's highly successful HBO network. Fraser Heston came up with an idea: why not approach Ted Turner with the idea of launching the network with a film version of A Man for All Seasons?

Ted Turner is quite an extraordinary guy. With TNT he was looking for a different audience than HBO was catering to at the time: a network that did not shy away from producing its own made-for-cable films, drawing from both classic and contemporary subjects. Of course, today all the movie channels routinely produce their own films, but in 1988 the idea was still quite revolutionary — and risky.

Fraser and I flew to Atlanta and pitched the idea to Ted. He liked it. In fact, he had only one condition: to have a cast that was a bit more recognizable to an American

Left: I played Sherlock Holmes in another film for Turner, *The Crucifer of Blood,* in 1992. Above: With the cast of "Chiefs."

I still remember reading *Treasure Island* to Fraser when he was a little boy. So when Ted Turner suggested we do another film together, *Treasure Island* popped up in Fraser's mind. Ted liked it.

audience than the cast we had in Britain. We readily agreed, for Ted was willing to provide the funds to get the people we had in mind. At the top of that list, naturally, was Sir John Gielgud. So I called him up. "John," I said, "I'm directing a film version of A Man for All Seasons, *and I want you to play Cardinal Wolsey in it.*"

"Oh, goodness me, Chuck," John said in his clipped British accent. "I really don't know. One does remember Orson Welles so well in the original film. He was so . . . so large, *you know.*"

"John, your reputation is ample enough to fill that role," I offered.

"Mmmmmm," said Gielgud, thinking this over. "It is *a very good part, isn't it?*"

"To be honest with you, I couldn't think of a better one-scene part in all of modern theater."

"Yes, yes, quite. Well, all right then. Very well, I'll do it."

With Sir John signed up, Vanessa Redgrave (who had played the role of Anne Boleyn in the 1966 version of A Man for all Seasons, *directed by Fred Zinnemann) graciously agreed to take on the role of Thomas More's wife, Alice. We shot at Pinewood *studios, which is my favorite studio, with absolutely wonderful stages and crew. Fraser was our producer, and Peter Snell, with whom I had done* Julius Caesar *and* Antony and Cleopatra, *worked as executive producer on the film. Since the cast knew the play well, including Vanessa and Sir John, I was able to shoot the film in the unbelievably short time of eighteen days.*

Heston still savors the memory of working together with these giants of the stage. Redgrave was later nominated for a Golden Globe award for her role as Mistress More, and Gielgud was nominated for an Ace Award. What's more, the film did very well for Turner—so much in fact, that Chuck and Fraser did two other projects for TNT: *Treasure Island* (1990) and *The Crucifer of Blood* (1991).

MEANWHILE, HOLLYWOOD WAS DOING rather well. Annual box-office revenues had steadily climbed from $2.9 billion in 1981 to as much as $5 billion in 1989. The film industry was on the rebound, propelled by a new generation of directors, including Steven Spielberg, George Lucas, and James Cameron. These young directors had tapped into a new genre that matched the frenzied pace of the roaring 1980s:

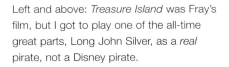

Left and above: *Treasure Island* was Fray's film, but I got to play one of the all-time great parts, Long John Silver, as a *real* pirate, not a Disney pirate.

fantasy epics with exotic drama and splashy, high-tech effects. In 1982, Spielberg's *E.T.* blew the top off the box office with an annual gross of nearly $200 million, a record closely matched by Lucas's *Star Wars* sequels in 1980 and 1983, and Tim Burton's *Batman* in 1989.

Hollywood's success did not go unnoticed in Japan, where the top consumer electronics firms were rolling in cash and eager to invest it in American entertainment. In 1989, Sony bought Columbia Pictures for more than $3 billion. One year later, Japanese electronics giant Matsushita purchased MCA–Universal for nearly double that amount, at an astounding price tag of $6 billion. Other Japanese corporations, including the NHK television group, also steered their investments into American-made motion pictures.

One such project was the $35 million science-fiction extravaganza *Solar Crisis* (1990), a co-production of Trimark Pictures with Gakken and NHK. The film, based on a novel by Takeshi Kawata, follows the attempt by a spaceship to fire a bomb into the sun to suppress a sun flare that will pulverize the earth. Heston accepted the part of Admiral "Skeet" Kelso, his first onscreen role in a science-

Above: As Henry Hooker in *Tombstone*, 1993.
Right: With Kurt Russell as Wyatt Earp.

fiction film since *Soylent Green* (although in the 1989 picture *Call from Space*, he gave voice to an alien creature). Unfortunately, *Solar Crisis* suffered from erratic distribution, and its box office in the United States was disappointing, even though the film was a hit in Japan.

In 1993, Heston appeared in two cameo roles in films that, in contrast to *Solar Crisis*, did very well: *Tombstone* and *Wayne's World 2* (both 1993). In *Tombstone*, directed by George Cosmatos, Heston played the role of Henry Hooker opposite Kurt Russell as Wyatt Earp and Val Kilmer as a whimsical Doc Holliday. Based on the events surrounding the legendary gunfight at the O.K. Corral, the picture was filmed on the actual locations in Tucson, Arizona. Distributed by Buena Vista Pictures, the film eventually grossed more than $100 million and became the first picture with Heston to be released on DVD. In *Wayne's World 2*, all Chuck had to do was to appear as himself.

In 1994, it was James Cameron's turn. He asked Heston to join his most ambitious action epic yet, *True Lies*, which featured a kinder, gentler Arnold Schwarzenegger in the leading role.

Cameron wanted me to play the role of Spencer Trilby, head of the C.I.A, who orders Arnold to retrieve a cache of nuclear weapons from the hands of terrorists. "Why do you want me in this picture?" I asked him.

"Simple." said the director, "I need a guy who can plausibly intimidate Arnold." (Not Arnold, but his character in the film.) I said, "If I can intimidate the Pharoah of Egypt, I can intimidate Arnold."*

True Lies required a record-high budget of more than $100 million dollars, which Jim Cameron used to explore a new level of photorealistic effects. Cameron wasn't apologetic. "We're using revolutionary technology," he said. "That translates into seamless digital imagery and nifty stunts. When a Harrier jet isn't flying around Miami, a villain is negotiating a breathless motorcycle leap from a hotel rooftop into a swimming pool across the street. Things go boom in the night. Jamie Lee performs a striptease. Arnold hurts people. There's something for everybody." It was a concise description of the type of films that Hollywood was staking its life on in the 1990s. Still, *True Lies* was not without humor. In one scene, an eye-patched Heston glowers at one of his agents, played by Grant Heslov.

"Who is this terrorist?" he asks.

"They call him the Sand Spider," Hezlov answers.

"Why?" Heston barks.

"I dunno," Hezlov responds. "Perhaps because it sounds scary."

True Lies ultimately grossed $360 million for Twentieth Century–Fox and Cameron's Lightstorm Entertainment.

FOR AS LONG AS HE CAN REMEMBER, Heston has been fascinated by the Five Books of Moses, the Pentateuch of the Old Testament. He studied it in preparation for his role as Moses in *The Ten Commandments*, and always nurtured the idea that here was a subject that deserved greater attention than the cursory quotations to which Hollywood pictures typically limit themselves. He was, above all, captivated by the literary qualities of this great classic, in the King James translation. "This side of Shakespeare," he says, "there is no finer writing in the English language." This is undoubtedly true, for the King James Bible, completed in 1611, ranks as the most popular English Bible of modern times.

Heston adapted the stories from the Pentateuch and the New Testament for television much in the same way he had adapted the plays of William Shakespeare.

We sold the program to the Arts & Entertainment network, and received a hefty advance from GoodTimes Video for the video rights. In fact, our only problem had to do with the locations. Fraser, and our producer John Stronach, wanted to shoot the film on location in Israel and Egypt, but we could not obtain permission from Egypt. Fortunately, John and Tony Westman, our cinematographer and director, had found a great location in Israel—the first century Roman amphitheater of Beil She'an, not far from the Sea of

Opposite: As Spencer Trilby, the one-eyed director of the C.I.A., in James Cameron's *True Lies*, 1994. "Why me?" I asked Jim. "I need someone who can plausibly intimidate Arnold Schwarzenegger," he replied. Left and above: On location for *The Bible* in Beit She'an, Israel. This side of Shakespeare, there's no better writing in the English language than in the King James Bible.

Galilee. It was a special thrill to perform the stories in a theater that, very likely, once held contemporaries of Jesus.

"Charlton Heston Presents the Bible" is a captivating four-hour miniseries—and from an acting perspective, a veritable tour de force. After its successful run on A&E, the series was released on video and also formed the basis for a twin set of multimedia CD-ROMs. Released in 1995, this was one of the first CD-ROM ventures to feature a major Hollywood actor, and a bemused Heston found himself in high demand at conferences devoted to multimedia technology.

IN 1996, FRASER HESTON was once again directing a film that reflected his love for the great outdoors. *Alaska* tells the story of a widower named Jake Barnes (played by Dirk Benedict, star of "Battlestar Galactica" and "The A-Team") who takes his teenage children from their native Chicago to the vast mountains of Alaska. A former airline pilot, Jake makes his living flying a Piper Cub to shuttle people and goods between the far-flung outlets of the mountain range. His daughter Jessie (Thora

Birch) adores the wilderness, but his son Sean (Vincent Kartheiser) has trouble adjusting. "Dad," he says, "you used to fly 747s, and now you deliver toilet paper." One night, Jake flies off in a storm to deliver an emergency package of medicine, but his plane never returns and is presumed lost in the mountains. Jessie and Sean set out to find him.

Alaska is a vintage Fraser Heston movie. The photography of the wide-open spaces and magnificent mountains of British Columbia (which doubled for Alaska) is breathtaking, thanks to cinematographer Tony Westman.

When the film opened on August 18, 1996, most reviews praised the glorious scenery and Heston's devilish performance as Perry, the evil poacher. "Under his son Fraser's direction, Charlton Heston adds some star power in one of his rare 'heavy' parts," wrote Carole Glines in *Box Office Magazine*; "it's amazing after all these years to still see the screen legend's physical vigor." *People Magazine*'s Ralph Novak wrote that "it makes for an engaging, energetic movie, thanks largely to the gorgeous scenery and the endearing polar bear Agee. . . . Not many

Opposite: Playing the bad guy can be great fun. Here as Perry in *Alaska,* 1996.
Above: With director Fraser on the set of *Alaska*, a vintage Fraser film.

films accessible to children are this tasteful, this action-packed and this much fun."
Internationally, *Alaska* was also well received. "This really is a film for the whole
family–rousing, touching, in the best sense wholesome entertainment," wrote Evan
Williams in *The Australian,* who confessed to a sense of awe in watching Chuck's
performance. "So powerful is the aura of nobility still clinging to the man that I
might have preferred him in the role of the father," Williams added, suggesting that
"the children's journey across swollen lakes and rapids offers thrilling reminders of
The African Queen."

CHARLTON HESTON IS AN ACTOR whose art is firmly rooted in William Shake-
speare. It was Shakespeare who opened Heston's eyes to his own talent; it was
Shakespeare that inspired him to write "my best screenplay," and it was with that same
Shakespeare play, *Antony and Cleopatra,* that Heston found his greatest fulfillment

as an actor and director. There is a touching symmetry to the fact that, in 1996, Heston's long career would be crowned with a performance in a Shakespeare film—and one that confirmed him, in the words of Sir Laurence Olivier, as "quite possibly the finest American Shakespearean actor of his time." It was the first attempt to film the complete text of Shakespeare's famous tragedy *Hamlet.* The man responsible for this mammoth undertaking was writer/director Kenneth Branagh, the British actor who had previously directed and starred in *Henry V* (1989) and *Much Ado About Nothing* (1993).

"It was a very ambitious project," Branagh says. "We were shooting on 65mm film, which takes much longer for setups. It's a format that was new to most people in the crew, for a 65mm film hasn't been shot in England since *Ryan's Daughter* in 1970. What's more, we're doing a movie of some three-and-a-half hours. That meant that I had to nail my colors to the mast and go in with a clear idea of how I wanted to shoot it and what I wanted this particular interpretation of *Hamlet* to be. That guided the way we went about casting people. If they didn't agree on kind of a base camp of how we were going to go about things, then we knew we probably shouldn't go forward."

The particular vision that Branagh was pursuing for this project caused Heston some distress. Branagh had assembled an "all-star cast" that included Julie Christie as Gertrude, Kate Winslet as Ophelia, and Derek Jacobi (Branagh's mentor, who once directed him in *Hamlet*) in the role of Claudius. With a keen eye to the commercial appeal of his four-hour film, Branagh had also signed Gérard Depardieu, Billy Crystal, and Robin Williams in cameo roles. "On this kind of project, even the agents would admit that it is usually better

Kenneth Branagh's *Hamlet,* 1996, was a wonderful experience featuring a truly magnificent cast, including Julie Christie, Derek Jacobi, Sir John Gielgud, Kate Winslet, Robin Williams, and Billy Crystal.

to go straight to the actor, with the notion that this is not something they would advise their clients to do from a financial point of view," Branagh says. "I also felt I could do it because this was not something that would require them for months and months." Indeed, some of the cameo roles, including those of Sir John Gielgud and Sir Richard Attenborough, required the actor's presence for not more than a day.

The exception was the part of the Player King. The "play within the play" and the long monologue of the Player King are routinely omitted on stage and in filmed versions of *Hamlet*, but Branagh knew that the scene is a critical turning point in the play.

The performance of the Player King as Gonzago pinpoints the very moment when Claudius reveals his guilt to the doubt-ridden Hamlet—giving the Danish prince undisputed proof that his uncle is guilty of the murder of his father. So, one day Ken calls me up. "I'd like you to play the part of the first player—the Player King," he says.

"I'd love to do it."

"Great," says Ken.

"You know, in all my Shakespeare performances I've always redacted the text a bit, using the various quartos and folios and so on, to get the strongest possible wording. If it's okay with you, I'd like to do that with the Player King text as well."

"I see," Ken says.

"Tell you what. I'll redact the text and send it to you. If you have any comments, just let me know."

So Kenneth hangs up, and I am left with the impression that he's agreed to this approach. For the next few months, until my call time at Pinewood Studios in England, I redact the Player King text, which as you

I played the Player King, leader of the troupe of actors that visits Elsinore Castle and provides Hamlet with the subterfuge to expose the murderous King. Most film and stage versions usually omit this part, which is regrettable, as it marks a pivotal moment in the play. The chance to play him in Ken's epic effort made it all the more rewarding.

know includes the monologue from the Play of Gonzago *and the "off-the-cuff" recitation from Virgil's* Aeneid, *in which Virgil mourns the death of Priam and Hecabe. I send my redaction to England, but got no word from Branagh. I had fully memorized my text and the shooting date was drawing near, so I gave Ken a call.*

"Chuck," he said, "I should've called you sooner. I really, really want to use the full text. I should've made that clear in the beginning."

Well, he was under a lot of stress. He was also the director, so I didn't press the issue. But the hardest thing was to go back and memorize a text that was similar but different from the one I had redacted, in such a short period of time.

It doesn't show on the screen. When the troupe of players arrive at Elsinore Castle, Heston's presence fills the vast mirrored hall. He accepts Hamlet's invitation to "give us a taste of your quality, a passionate speech," and steps onto the dais. His lifts his chin, that characteristic Heston gesture that recalls his many other Shakespearean orations, and raises his hand. The famous voice booms through the hall:

> But if the gods themselves did see her the
> When she saw Pyrrhus make malicious sport
> In mincing with his sword her husband's limbs,
> The instant burst of clamour that she made,
> Unless things mortal move them not at all,
> Would have made milch the burning eyes of heaven
> And passion in the gods . . .

The Player King bows his head, overcome with passion. Hamlet is deeply moved. Later, in his room, Hamlet berates his own cowardice and passivity, wondering how the Player King could "force his soul so to his own conceit . . . tears in his eyes . . . a broken voice!" Scored with the rousing music of Patrick Doyle, this great scene leaves the audience no less impressed.

It was great to be at Pinewood once again and play in this magnificent production. Hamlet is such a wonderful story. My role of the Player King had a special significance, for the "play-within-the-play" scene is usually cut back to just the mime. It was fascinating to explore the full role, particularly to work again with Rosemary Harris (the Player Queen). Ken empathizes wonderfully with his actors. He knows where he's going and how to get there. He prods and pushes—and I like directors who demand a lot.

The critics gave Heston high marks for his moving performance. "One of the surprises of this uncut version of *Hamlet* is the crucial role of the play within the play," Roger Ebert wrote in the *Chicago Sun-Times*. "Charlton Heston is magnificently assured as the Player King." Writing for *USA Today*, Mike Clark found that

"Charlton Heston is a shot in the arm as the Player King." For *Time*'s Richard Corliss, the film was "big, pretty, vigorous, thoughtful." Accolades were heard as far as Europe, where George Waser wrote in the *Neue Zürcher Zeitung* that Heston's performance was nothing short of "extraordinary, evoking the style of a great Victorian actor."

AS HE APPROACHES HIS SEVENTY-FIFTH YEAR, Charlton Heston shows no signs of slowing down. In the wake of his best-selling autobiography *In the Arena*, he's published a book of personal advice to his grandson Jack Heston, entitled *To Be a Man: Letters to My Grandson*, and is working on a new book project. In 1997, he narrated the Disney animated feature *Hercules*, and in January 1998, he appeared on the hit television series "Friends." In election campaigns, he tirelessly stumps along with the candidate of his choice (usually of the Republican persuasion), and never shuns the spotlight of a news camera to articulate his passionately held beliefs. While he is on the campaign trail, reporters invariably ask him why he himself has not taken a more active part on the political scene. He smiles and replies with his stock answer that, in fact, he has been many political figures—including presidents. But in truth, where would he find the time? With a continuing flurry of activity in acting, writing, and public service, Charlton Heston is too busy being the elder statesman of Hollywood.

With family. From left, Carleton, Holly, Lydia, Jack, Marilyn, Fray, and me.

FILMOGRAPHY

PEER GYNT (1941)
Bradley Films

Director: David Bradley
Producer: David Bradley
Screenplay: Henrik Ibsen, adapted by
David Bradley
Cinematography: David Bradley
Principal cast: Charlton Heston as Peer
Gynt; Betty Barton as Ingrid; Kathryne
Elfstrom as Solveig.
Notes: Re-released in 1965 with soundtrack
featuring music from the *Peer Gynt Suite* by
Edvard Grieg

JULIUS CAESAR (1950)
Avon Productions, Inc.

Director: David Bradley
Producer: David Bradley
Screenplay: William Shakespeare, adapted by
David Bradley
Cinematography: Louis McMahon
Musical score: John Becker
Principal cast: Charlton Heston as Marc
Antony, David Bradley as Brutus, Grosvenor
Glenn as Cassius, Harold Tasker as Julius
Caesar

DARK CITY (1950)
Paramount Pictures

Director: William Dieterle
Producer: Hal B. Wallis
Screenplay: Ketti Frings, John Meredyth
Lucas, and Larry Marcus, based on the story
"No Escape"
Cinematography: Victor Milner
Musical score: Franz Waxman
Principal cast: Charlton Heston as Danny
Haley, Lizabeth Scott as Fran Garland, Don
DeFore as Arthur Winant, Viveca Lindfors as
Victoria Winant, Jack Webb as Augie
Note: *Dark City* was Charlton Heston's
Hollywood debut
Video: Not released for home video

THE SAVAGE (1952)
Paramount Pictures

Director: George Marshall
Producer: Mel Epstein
Screenplay: Sydney Boehm
Cinematography: John F. Seitz
Musical score: Paul Sawtell
Principal cast: Charlton Heston as
Warbonnet (Jim Aherne, Jr.), Angela Clarke as
Pehangi, Peter Hanson as Lieutenant Weston
Hathersall, Ian MacDonald as Yellow Eagle,
Susan Morrow as Tally Hathersall, Howard
Negly as Colonel Ellis Donald Porter, Orley
Lindgren as Warbonnet as a boy
Video: Not released for home video

RUBY GENTRY (1952)
20th Century–Fox

Director: King Vidor
Producers: Joseph Bernhard and King Vidor
Screenplay: Silvia Richards
Cinematography: Russell Harlan
Musical score: Heinz Roemheld
Principal cast: Charlton Heston as Boake
Tackman, Jennifer Jones as Ruby Gentry, Karl
Malden as Jim Gentry, Tom Tully as Jud
Corey, Josephine Hutchinson as Letitia Gentry
Video: Available on videocassette

THE GREATEST SHOW ON EARTH
(1952)
Paramount Pictures

Director: Cecil B. DeMille
Producer: Cecil B. DeMille
Screenplay: Fredric M. Frank, Barre Lyndon,
Theodore St. John, and Frank Cavett
Cinematography: George Barnes,
J. Peverell Marley, and Wallace Kelley
Musical score: Victor Young
Principal cast: Charlton Heston as Brad
Braden, Betty Hutton as Holly, Cornel Wilde
as "The Great Sebastian," Dorothy Lamour as
Phyllis, Gloria Grahame as Angel, Henry
Wilcoxon as Gregory of the FBI, James
Stewart as Buttons the Clown
Video: Available on videocassette and laser disc

THE PRESIDENT'S LADY (1953)
20th Century–Fox

Director: Henry Levin
Producer: Sol C. Siegel
Screenplay: John Patrick
Cinematography: Leo Tover
Musical score: Alfred Newman
Principal cast: Charlton Heston as
President Andrew Jackson, Susan Hayward
as Rachel Donelson Robards Jackson,
John McIntire as Jack Overton, Fay Bainter
as Mrs. Donelson, Whitfield Connor as
Lewis Robards
Video: Available on videocassette

PONY EXPRESS (1953)
Paramount Pictures

Director: Jerry Hopper
Producer: Nat Holt
Screenplay: Charles Marquis Warren
Cinematography: Ray Rennahan
Musical score: Paul Sawtell
Principal cast: Charlton Heston as Buffalo
Bill Cody, Rhonda Fleming as Evelyn
Hastings, Jan Sterling as Denny Russell,
Forrest Tucker as Wild Bill Hickok, Michael
Moore as Rance Hastings
Video: Available on videocassette

ARROWHEAD (1953)
Paramount Pictures

Director: Charles Marquis Warren
Producer: Nat Holt
Screenplay: Charles Marquis Warren
Cinematography: Ray Rennahan
Musical score: Paul Sawtell
Principal cast: Charlton Heston as Ed
Bannon, Jack Palance as Toriano, Katy Jurado
as Nita, Brian Keith as Captain Bill North,
Mary Sinclair as Lee Wilson, Richard
Shannon as Lieutenant Kirk
Video: Available on videocassette and laser disc

BAD FOR EACH OTHER (1953)
Columbia Pictures

Director: Irving Rapper
Producer: William Fadiman
Screenplay: Irving Wallace and Horace McCoy
Cinematography: Frank Planer
Musical score: Mischa Bakaleinikoff
Principal cast: Charlton Heston as Dr. Tom Owen, Lizabeth Scott as Helen Curtis, Dianne Foster as Joan Lasher, Mildred Dunnock as Mrs. Owen, Arthur Franz as Dr. Jim Crowley, Lydia Clarke as Rita Thornburg
Video: Not released for home video

THE SECRET OF THE INCAS (1954)
Paramount Pictures

Director: Jerry Hopper
Producer: Mel Epstein
Screenplay: Sydney Boehm and Ranald MacDougall
Cinematography: Lionel Lindon
Musical score: David Buttolph
Principal cast: Charlton Heston as Harry Steele, Robert Young as Stanley Moore, Nicole Maurey as Elena Antonoescu, Yma Sumac as Kori Tica, Thomas Mitchell as Ed Morgan, Glenda Farrell as Mrs. Winston
Video: Not released for home video

THE NAKED JUNGLE (1954)
Paramount Pictures

Director: Byron Haskin
Producers: George Pal; Frank Freeman, Jr., associate producer
Screenplay: Philip Yordan and Ranald MacDougall
Cinematography: Ernest Laszlo
Musical score: Daniele Amfitheatrof
Principal cast: Charlton Heston as Christopher Leiningen, Eleanor Parker as Joanna Leiningen, Abraham Sofaer as Incacha, William Conrad as the Commissioner
Video: Available on videocassette and laser disc

THE PRIVATE WAR OF MAJOR BENSON (1955)
Universal International Pictures

Director: Jerry Hopper
Producer: Howard Pine
Screenplay: William Roberts and Richard Alan Simmons
Cinematography: Harold Lipstein

Musical score: Joseph Gershenson
Principal cast: Charlton Heston as Major Bernard "Barney" Benson, Julie Adams as Kay Lambert, William Demarest as John, Tim Considine as Cadet Sgt. Hibler, Sal Mineo as Cadet Col. Sylvester Dusik
Video: Not released for home video

LUCY GALLANT (1955)
Paramount Pictures

Director: Robert Parrish
Producers: William H. Pine and William C. Thomas
Screenplay: John Lee Mahin and Winston Miller
Cinematography: Lionel Lindon
Musical score: Van Cleave
Principal cast: Charlton Heston as Casey Cole, Jane Wyman as Lucy Gallant, Claire Trevor as Lady MacBeth, William Demarest as Charles Madden
Video: Not released for home video

THE FAR HORIZONS (1955)
Paramount Pictures

Director: Rudolph Maté
Producers: William H. Pine and William C. Thomas
Screenplay: Winston Miller and Edmund H. North
Cinematography: Daniel L. Fapp
Musical score: Hans J. Salter
Principal cast: Charlton Heston as William Clark, Fred MacMurray as Merriwether Lewis, Donna Reed as Sacajawea, Barbara Hale as Julia Hancock, William Demarest as Sgt. Cass, Alan Reed as Charboneau
Video: Not released for home video

THREE VIOLENT PEOPLE (1956)
Paramount Pictures

Director: Rudolph Maté
Producer: Hugh Brown
Screenplay: James Edward Grant
Cinematography: Loyal Griggs
Musical score: William Scharf
Principal cast: Charlton Heston as Colt Saunders, Anne Baxter as Lorna Hunter Saunders, Gilbert Roland as Innocencio, Tom Tryon as Cinch Saunders, Forrest Tucker as Deputy Commissioner Cable, Elaine Strich as Ruby LaSalle, Bruce Bennett as Commissioner Harrison
Video: Available on videocassette

THE TEN COMMANDMENTS (1956)
Paramount Pictures

Director: Cecil B. DeMille
Producer: Cecil B. DeMille
Screenplay: Aeneas MacKenzie, Jesse L. Lasky, Jr., Jack Gariss, and Fredric M. Frank
Cinematography: Loyal Griggs
Musical score: Elmer Bernstein
Principal cast: Charlton Heston as Moses, Yul Brynner as Ramses, Anne Baxter as Nefretiri, Edward G. Robinson as Dathan, Yvonne De Carlo as Sephora, Debra Paget as Lilia, Cedric Hardwicke as Sethi, Nina Foch as Brithiah, Martha Scott as Yochabel, John Carradine as Aaron, Henry Wilcoxon as Pentaur, Vincent Price as Baka
Video: Available on videocassette and laser disc

THE BUCCANEER (1958)
Paramount Pictures

Director: Anthony Quinn
Producer: Henry Wilcoxon
Screenplay: Jesse L. Lasky, Jr. and Berenice Mosk, based on several earlier screenplays by Harold Lamb, Edwin Justis Mayer, and C. Gardner Sullivan
Cinematography: Loyal Griggs
Musical score: Elmer Bernstein
Principal cast: Charlton Heston as General Andrew Jackson, Yul Brynner as Jean Lafitte, Claire Bloom as Bonnie Brown, Charles Boyer as Dominique You, Inger Stevens as Annette Claiborne, E. G. Marshall as Governor Claiborne, Lorne Greene as Mercier
Video: Available on videocassette and laser disc

THE BIG COUNTRY (1958)
United Artists/Anthony-Worldwide

Director: William Wyler
Producers: William Wyler and Gregory Peck
Screenplay: James R. Webb, Sy Bartlett, and Robert Wilder, adapted by Jessamyn West and Robert Wyler
Cinematography: Franz F. Planer
Musical score: Jerome Moross
Principal cast: Gregory Peck as James McKay, Jean Simmons as Julie Maragon, Carroll Baker as Patricia Terrill, Charlton Heston as Steve Leech, Burl Ives as Rufus Hannassey, Charles Bickford as Major Terrill, Chuck Connors as Buck Hannassey
Video: Available on videocassette

TOUCH OF EVIL (1958)
Universal International

Director: Orson Welles
Producer: Albert Zugsmith
Screenplay: Orson Welles
Cinematography: Russell Metty
Musical score: Henry Mancini
Principal cast: Charlton Heston as Ramon Miguel "Mike" Vargas, Janet Leigh as Susan Vargas, Orson Welles as Hank Quinlan, Joseph Calleia as Pete Menzies, Akim Tamiroff as "Uncle" Joe Grandi. Cameo appearances by Marlene Dietrich and Joseph Cotten.
Video: Available on videocassette and laser disc

THE WRECK OF THE MARY DEARE (1959)
Metro-Goldwyn-Mayer

Director: Michael Anderson
Producer: Julian Blaustein
Screenplay: Eric Ambler
Cinematography: Joseph Ruttenberg and Fred Young
Musical score: George Duning
Principal cast: Gary Cooper as Gideon Patch, Charlton Heston as John Sands, Michael Redgrave as Mr. Hyland, Emlyn Williams as Sir Wilfred Falcett, Cecil Parker as The Chairman, Richard Harris as Higgins
Video: Available on videocassette and laser disc

BEN-HUR (1959)
Metro-Goldwyn-Mayer

Director: William Wyler
Producer: Sam Zimbalist
Screenplay: Karl Tunberg
Cinematography: Robert L. Surtees
Musical score: Miklos Rozsa
Principal cast: Charlton Heston as Judah Ben-Hur, Jack Hawkins as Quintas, Haya Harareet as Esther, Stephen Boyd as Messala, Hugh Griffith as Sheik Ilderim, Martha Scott as Miriam, Cathy O'Donnell as Tirzah, Frank Thring as Pontius Pilate
Video: Available on videocassette and laser disc
Note: Released on letterbox videocassette in 1996

EL CID (1961)
Dear Film/Allied Artists Pictures

Director: Anthony Mann
Producers: Samuel Bronston, with associate producers Jaime Prades and Michael Waszynski
Screenplay: Philip Yordan and Fredric M. Frank

Cinematography: Robert Krasker
Musical score: Miklos Rozsa
Principal cast: Charlton Heston as Rodrigo Diaz de Bivar, Sophia Loren as Chimene, Raf Vallone as Count Ordonez, Genevieve Page as Princess Urraca, John Fraser as Prince Alfonso, Gary Raymond as Prince Sancho, Hurd Hatfield as Arias, Massimo Serato as Fanez
Video: Available on videocassette and laser disc

DIAMOND HEAD (1962)
Columbia Pictures

Director: Guy Green
Producer: Jerry Bresler
Screenplay: Marguerite Roberts
Cinematography: Sam Leavitt
Musical score: John Williams
Principal cast: Charlton Heston as Richard Howland, Yvette Mimieux as Sloan Howland, George Chakiris as Dr. Dean Kahana, France Nuyen as Mei Chen, James Darren as Paul Kahana
Video: Available on videocassette and laser disc

THE PIGEON THAT TOOK ROME (1962)
Paramount Pictures

Director: Melville Shavelson
Producer: Melville Shavelson
Screenplay: Melville Shavelson
Cinematography: Daniel L. Fapp
Musical score: Alessandro Cicognini
Principal cast: Charlton Heston as Captain Paul MacDougall, Elsa Martinelli as Antonella Massimo, Harry Guardino as Sergeant Joseph Contini, Brian Donlevy as Colonel Sherman Harrington
Video: Not released for home video

55 DAYS AT PEKING (1963)
Samuel Bronston Productions

Director: Nicholas Ray
Producer: Samuel Bronston
Screenplay: Bernard Gordon and Philip Yordan
Cinematography: Jack Hildyard
Musical score: Dimitri Tiomkin
Principal cast: Charlton Heston as Major Matt Lewis, David Niven as Sir Arthur Robertson, Ava Gardner as Baroness Natalie Ivanoff, Flora Robson as Dowager Empress Tzu Hsi, Elizabeth Sellars as Lady Sarah Robertson, Nicholas Ray as the American Minister
Video: Available on videocassette and laser disc

THE AGONY AND THE ECSTASY (1965)
20th Century–Fox

Director: Carol Reed
Producer: Carol Reed
Screenplay: Philip Dunne
Cinematography: Leon Shamroy
Musical score: Alex North; choral music by Franco Potenza
Principal cast: Charlton Heston as Michelangelo, Rex Harrison as Pope Julius II, Diane Cilento as Contessina de Medici, Harry Andrews as Bramante, Alberto Lupo as Duke of Urbino, Adolfo Celi as Giovanni de Medici
Video: Available on videocassette and laser disc

THE GREATEST STORY EVER TOLD (1965)
United Artists

Director: George Stevens
Producer: George Stevens
Screenplay: James Lee Barrett and George Stevens
Cinematography: William C. Mellor and Loyal Griggs
Musical score: Alfred Newman
Principal cast: Max von Sydow as Jesus, Dorothy McGuire as Mary, Robert Loggia as Joseph, Charlton Heston as John the Baptist, Robert Blake as Simon the Zealot, David Hedison as Philip, Roddy McDowall as Matthew, Sidney Poitier as Simon of Cyrene
Video: Available on videocassette and laser disc

MAJOR DUNDEE (1965)
Columbia Pictures

Director: Sam Peckinpah
Producer: Jerry Bresler
Screenplay: Harry Julian Fink, Oscar Saul, and Sam Peckinpah
Cinematography: Sam Leavitt
Musical score: Daniele Amfitheatrof
Principal cast: Charlton Heston as Major Amos Dundee, Richard Harris as Captain Benjamin Tyreen, Jim Hutton as Lieutenant Graham, James Coburn as Samuel T. Potts, Senta Berger as Teresa Santiago, Ben Johnson as Sergeant Chillum
Video: Available on videocassette

THE WAR LORD (1965)
Universal Pictures

Director: Franklin J. Schaffner
Producer: Walter Seltzer
Screenplay: John Collier and Millard Kaufman

Cinematography: Russell Metty
Musical score: Jerome Moross
Principal cast: Charlton Heston as
Chrysagon, Richard Boone as Bors, Rosemary
Forsyth as Bronwyn, Maurice Evans as Priest,
Guy Stockwell as Draco, Niall MacGinnis as
Odins, Henry Wilcoxon as Frisian King
Video: Available on videocassette

KHARTOUM (1966)
United Artists

Director: Basil Dearden
Producer: Julian Blaustein
Screenplay: Robert Ardrey
Cinematography: Edward Scaife
Musical score: Frank Cordell
Principal cast: Charlton Heston as General
Charles Gordon, Laurence Olivier as the
Mahdi, Richard Johnson as Colonel J.D.H.
Stewart, Ralph Richardson as William
Gladstone, Alexander Knox as Sir Evelyn
Baring, Zia Mohyeddin as Zobeir Pasha
Video: Available on videocassette and laser disc

PLANET OF THE APES (1968)
20th Century–Fox

Director: Franklin J. Schaffner
Producer: Arthur P. Jacobs
Screenplay: Michael Wilson and Rod Serling
Cinematography: Leon Shamroy
Musical score: Jerry Goldsmith
Principal cast: Charlton Heston as George
Taylor, Roddy McDowall as Cornelius, Kim
Hunter as Zira, Maurice Evans as Dr. Zaius,
James Whitmore as President of the
Assembly, Linda Harrison as Nova, Robert
Gunner as Landon
Video: Available on videocassette and laser disc

COUNTERPOINT (1968)
Universal Pictures

Director: Ralph Nelson
Producer: Dick Berg
Screenplay: James Lee and Joel Oliansky
Cinematography: Russell Metty
Musical score: Bronislaw Kaper
Principal cast: Charlton Heston as Lionel
Evans, Maximilian Schell as General
Schiller, Kathryn Hays as Annabelle Rice,
Anton Diffring as Colonel Arndt, Leslie
Nielsen as Victor Rice
Video: Not released for home video

WILL PENNY (1968)
Paramount Pictures

Director: Tom Gries
Producer: Fred Engel and Walter Seltzer
Screenplay: Tom Gries
Cinematography: Lucien Ballard
Musical score: David Raksin
Principal cast: Charlton Heston as Will
Penny, Joan Hackett as Catherine Allen,
Donald Pleasence as Preacher Quint, Lee
Majors as Blue, Bruce Dern as Rafe Quint, Ben
Johnson as Alex, Lydia Clarke as Mrs. Fraker
Video: Available on videocassette and laser disc

NUMBER ONE (1969)
Walter Seltzer Productions

Director: Tom Gries
Producer: Walter Seltzer
Screenplay: David Moessinger
Cinematography: Michel Hugo
Musical score: Dominic Frontiere
Principal cast: Charlton Hest as Ron
"Cat" Catlin, Jessica Walters as Julie
Catlan, Bruce Dern as Richie Fowler,
John Randolph as Coach Jim Southend,
Diane Muldaur as Ann Marley
Video: Not released for home video

JULIUS CAESAR (1970)
Commonwealth United Entertainment

Director: Stuart Burge
Producer: Peter Snell
Screenplay: Robert Furnival
Cinematography: Ken Higgins
Musical score: Michael Lewis
Principal cast: Charlton Heston as Marc
Antony, Jason Robards, Jr. as Brutus, John
Gielgud as Julius Caesar, Richard Johnson as
Cassius, Robert Vaughn as Casca, Richard
Chamberlain as Octavius Caesar, Diana Rigg
as Portia, Christopher Lee as Artemidorus
Video: Available on videocassette and laser disc

THE HAWAIIANS (1970)
United Artists/Mirisch

Director: Tom Gries
Producer: Walter Mirisch
Screenplay: James R. Webb
Cinematography: Philip Lathrop and
Lucien Ballard
Musical score: Henry Mancini
Principal cast: Charlton Heston as Whip
Hoxworth, Tina Chen as Nyuk Tsin, Geraldine
Chaplin as Purity Hoxworth, Mako as Mun Ki
Video: Not released for home video

BENEATH THE PLANET
OF THE APES (1970)
20th Century–Fox

Director: Ted Post
Producer: Arthur P. Jacobs
Screenplay: Mort Abrahams and Paul Dehn
Cinematography: Milton R. Krasner
Musical score: Leonard Rosenman
Principal cast: James Franciscus as Brent,
Charlton Heston as Taylor, Kim Hunter as
Dr. Zira, Maurice Evans as Dr. Zaius, Linda
Harrison as Nova, Paul Richards as Mendez,
Victor Buono as Adiposo
Video: Available on videocassette and laser disc

THE OMEGA MAN (1971)
Warner Bros.

Director: Boris Sagal
Producer: Walter Seltzer
Screenplay: John William Corrington and
Joyce H. Corrington
Cinematography: Russell Metty
Musical score: Ron Grainer
Principal cast: Charlton Heston as
Robert Neville, Anthony Zerbe as Matthias,
Rosalind Cash as Lisa, Paul Koslo as
Dutch, Eric Laneuville as Richie,
Lincoln Kilpatrick as Zachary
Video: Available on videocassette

SKYJACKED (1972)
Metro-Goldwyn-Mayer

Director: John Guillermin
Producer: Walter Seltzer
Screenplay: Stanley R. Greenberg
Cinematography: Harry Stradling, Jr.
Musical score: Perry Botkin, Jr.
Principal cast: Charlton Heston as Captain
Henry "Hank" O'Hara, Yvette Mimieux as
Angela Thacher, James Brolin as Jerome K.
Weber, Susan Dey as Elly Brewster, Mariette
Hartley as Harriet Stevens
Video: Available on videocassette and laser disc

ANTONY AND CLEOPATRA (1973)
Transac, Izaro Films, Folio Films, Rank

Director: Charlton Heston
Producer: Peter Snell
Screenplay: Charlton Heston
Cinematography: Rafael Pacheco
Musical score: John Scott

Principal cast: Charlton Heston as Antony, Hildegard Neil as Cleopatra, Eric Porter as Enobarbus, John Castle as Octavius, Fernando Rey as Lepidus
Note: Fraser Clarke Heston is the Assistant Director.
Video: Available on videocassette

THE CALL OF THE WILD (1973)
Metro-Goldwyn-Mayer

Director: Ken Annakin
Producer: Harry Alan Towers
Screenplay: Peter Welbeck (Harry Alan Towers)
Cinematography: John Cabrera
Musical score: Carlo Rustichelli
Principal cast: Charlton Heston as John Thornton, Michele Mercier as Calliope Laurent, Raimund Harmstorf as Pete, George Eastman as Black Burton
Video: Available on videocassette

SOYLENT GREEN (1973)
Metro-Goldwyn-Mayer

Director: Richard Fleischer
Producer: Walter Seltzer and Russell Thatcher
Screenplay: Stanley R. Greenberg
Cinematography: Richard H. Kline
Musical score: Fred Myrow
Principal cast: Charlton Heston as Police Detective Thorn, Leigh Taylor-Young as Shirl, Chuck Connors as Tab Fielding, Joseph Cotten as William Simonson, Brock Peters as Hatcher, Paula Kelly as Martha, Edward G. Robinson as Sol Roth, Stephen Young as Gilbert
Video: Available on videocassette and laser disc

THE THREE MUSKETEERS (1973)
(The Queen's Diamonds)
20th Century–Fox

Director: Richard Lester
Producer: Alexander Salkind
Screenplay: George MacDonald Fraser
Cinematography: David Watkin
Musical score: Michel Legrand
Principal cast: Michael York as d'Artagnan, Oliver Reed as Athos, Raquel Welch as Constance Bonancieux, Richard Chamberlain as Aramis, Frank Finlay as Porthos, Charlton Heston as Cardinal

Richelieu, Faye Dunaway as Milady de Winter, Christopher Lee as Rochefort
Video: Available on videocassette
Note: Newly released on videocassette in 1998

EARTHQUAKE (1974)
Universal Pictures

Director: Mark Robson
Producer: Mark Robson
Screenplay: George Fox and Mario Puzo
Cinematography: Philip H. Lathrop
Musical score: John Williams
Principal cast: Charlton Heston as Stuart Graff, Ava Gardner as Remy Graff, George Kennedy as Lew Slade, Lorne Greene as Sam Royce, Genevieve Bujold as Denise Marshall, Victoria Principal as Rosa Amici, Walter Matthau as Drunk (as Walter Matuschanskayasky)
Video: Available on videocassette and laser disc

AIRPORT 1975 (1974)
Universal Pictures

Director: Jack Smight
Producer: William Frye
Screenplay: Don Ingalls
Cinematography: Philip H. Lathrop
Musical score: John Cacavas
Principal cast: Charlton Heston as Alan Murdock, Karen Black as Nancy, George Kennedy as Joe Patroni, Efrem Zimbalist, Jr. as Stacy, Susan Clark as Mrs. Patroni, Helen Reddy as Sister Ruth, Linda Blair as Janice Abbott, Dana Andrews as Scott Freeman, Roy Thinnes as Urias, Gloria Swanson as herself
Video: Available on videocassette

THE FOUR MUSKETEERS (1975)
(The Revenge of Milady)
20th Century–Fox

Director: Richard Lester
Producer: Alexander Salkind and Michael Salkind
Screenplay: George MacDonald Fraser
Cinematography: David Watkin
Musical score: Lalo Schifren
Principal cast: Oliver Reed as Athos, Raquel Welch as Constance Bonancieux, Richard Chamberlain as Aramis, Michael York as d'Artagnan, Frank Finlay as Porthos, Simon Ward as Duke of Buckingham, Christopher Lee as Rochefort, Faye Dunaway as Milady de

Winter, Charlton Heston as Richelieu, Geraldine Chaplin as Anne of Austria
Video: Available on videocassette
Notes: *The Four Musketeers* was split off from the 1973 production of *The Three Musketeers* and released as a separate sequel two years later. Several actors sued but a settlement was reached. *Four Musketeers* was again released on videocassette in 1998.

TWO MINUTE WARNING (1976)
Universal Pictures

Director: Larry Peerce
Producer: Edward S. Feldman
Screenplay: Edward Hume
Cinematography: Gerald Hirschfeld
Musical score: Charles Fox
Principal cast: Charlton Heston as Captain Peter Holly, John Cassavetes as Button, Martin Balsam as McKeever, Beau Bridges as Mike Ramsay, David Janssen as Steve, Jack Klugman as Sandman, Gena Rowlands as Janet
Video: Available on videocassette and laser disc

THE BATTLE OF MIDWAY (1976)
Universal Pictures

Director: Jack Smight
Producer: Walter Mirisch
Screenplay: Donald S. Sanford
Cinematography: Harry Stradling, Jr.
Musical score: John Williams
Principal cast: Charlton Heston as Captain Matt Garth, Henry Fonda as Admiral Chester W. Nimitz, James Coburn as Captain Vinton Maddox, Glenn Ford as Rear Admiral Raymond A. Spruance, Hal Holbrook as Commander Joseph Rochefort, Jr., Toshiro Mifune as Admiral Isoroku Yamamoto, Robert Mitchum as Admiral William F. "Bull" Halsey, Jr., Cliff Robertson as Commander Carl Jessop, Robert Wagner as Lieutenant Commander Ernest L. Blake
Video: Available on videocassette and laser disc

THE LAST HARD MEN (1976)
20th Century–Fox

Director: Andrew V. McLaglen
Producers: Russell Thatcher and Walter Seltzer
Screenplay: Guerdon Trueblood
Cinematography: Duke Callaghan

Musical score: Jerry Goldsmith
Principal cast: Charlton Heston as Sam Burgade, James Coburn as Zach Provo, Barbara Hershey as Susan Burgade, Christopher Mitchum as Hal Brickman, Robert Donner as Lee Roy
Video: Not released for home video

GRAY LADY DOWN (1978)
Universal Pictures

Director: David Greene
Producer: Walter Mirisch
Screenplay: James Whittaker and Howard Sackler
Cinematography: Steven Larner
Musical score: Jerry Fielding
Principal cast: Charlton Heston as Captain Paul Blanchard, David Carradine as Captain Donald R. Gates, Stacy Keach as Captain Harold "Ben" Bennett, Ned Beatty as Mickey, Ronny Cox as Commander Samuelson
Video: Available on videocassette

CROSSED SWORDS (1978)
(aka The Prince and the Pauper)
Warner Bros.

Director: Richard Fleischer
Producer: Pierre Spengler
Screenplay: George MacDonald Fraser, Berta Dominguez D., Pierre Spengler
Cinematography: Jack Cardiff
Musical score: Maurice Jarre
Principal cast: Charlton Heston as King Henry VIII, Oliver Reed as Miles Hendon, Raquel Welch as Lady Edith, Mark Lester as Edward/Tom, Ernest Borgnine as John Canty, George C. Scott as The Ruffler, Rex Harrison as Duke of Norfolk
Video: Available on videocassette

THE AWAKENING (1980)
EMI/Orion Pictures

Director: Mike Newell
Producer: Robert H. Solo
Screenplay: Chris Bryant, Clive Exton, and Allan Scott
Cinematography: Jack Cardiff
Musical score: Claude Bolling
Principal cast: Charlton Heston as Matthew Corbeck, Susannah York as Jane Turner, Jill Townsend as Anne Corbeck, Stephanie Zimbalist as Margaret Corbeck, Patrick Drury as Paul Whittier, Bruce Myers as Dr. Khalid
Video: Available on videocassette and laser disc

THE MOUNTAIN MEN (1980)
Columbia Pictures

Director: Richard Lang
Producers: Martin Shafer, Martin Ransohoff, and Andrew Scheinman
Screenplay: Fraser Clarke Heston
Cinematography: Michael Hugo
Musical score: Michel Legrand
Principal cast: Charlton Heston as Bill Tyler, Brian Keith as Henry Frapp, Victoria Racimo as Running Moon, Seymour Cassel as La Bont, John Glover as Nathan Wyeth, David Ackroyd as Medicine Wolf
Video: Available on videocassette and laser disc

MOTHER LODE (1982)
Agamemnon Films

Director: Charlton Heston
Producers: Peter Snell and Fraser Clarke Heston
Screenplay: Fraser Clarke Heston
Cinematography: Richard Leiterman
Musical score: Kenneth Wannberg
Principal cast: Charlton Heston as Silas McGee/Ian McGee, Nick Mancuso as Jean Dupré, Kim Basinger as Andrea Spalding, John Marley as Elijha
Video: Available on videocassette

A MAN FOR ALL SEASONS (1988)
Turner Network Television

Director: Charlton Heston
Producer: Fraser Clarke Heston
Screenplay: Robert Bolt
Principal cast: Charlton Heston as Sir Thomas More, John Gielgud as Cardinal Wolsey, Roy Kinnear as The Chorus, Vanessa Redgrave as Mistress Alice More
Video: Available on videocassette

SOLAR CRISIS (1990)
Trimark/Gakken/NHK

Director: Richard C. Sarafian
(as Allen Smithee)
Producer: George Jenson
Screenplay: Joe Gannon and Crispan Bolt
Cinematography: Russell Carpenter
Musical score: Maurice Jarre
Principal cast: Charlton Heston as Admiral "Skeet" Kelso, Tim Matheson as Steve Kelso, Peter Boyle as Arnold Teague, Annabel

Schofield as Alex Noffe, Jack Palance as Travis, Dorian Harewood as Borg
Video: Available on videocassette and laser disc

TREASURE ISLAND (1990)
Turner Network Television

Director: Fraser Clarke Heston
Screenplay: Fraser Clarke Heston
Cinematography: Robert Steadman
Principal cast: Charlton Heston as Long John Silver, Christian Bale as Jim Hawkins, Oliver Reed as Captain Billy Bones, Christopher Lee Blind Pew, Richard Johnson as Squire Trelawney
Video: Available on videocassette and laser disc
Note: Theatrically released in Europe by Warner Bros.

WAYNE'S WORLD 2 (1993)
Paramount Pictures

Director: Stephen Surjik
Producer: Lorne Michaels
Screenplay: Mike Myers, Bonnie Turner, and Terry Turner
Cinematography: Francis Kenny
Musical score: Carter Burwell
Principal cast: Mike Myers as Wayne Campbell, Dana Carvey as Garth Algar, Lee Tergesen as Terry, Dan Bell as Neil, Tia Carrere as Cassandra, Heather Locklear as Herself, Rip Taylor as Himself, Kim Basinger as Honey Horne, Charlton Heston as Good Actor
Video: Available on videocassette, laser disc, and VideoCD

TOMBSTONE (1993)
Cinergi Productions

Director: George P. Cosmatos
Producers: James Jacks, Sean Daniel, and Bob Misiorowski
Screenplay: Kevin Jarre
Cinematography: William A. Fraker
Musical score: Bruce Broughton
Principal cast: Kurt Russell as Wyatt Earp, Val Kilmer as Doc Holliday, Sam Elliott as Virgil Earp, Bill Paxton as Morgan Earp, Powers Boothe as Curly Bill, Michael Biehn as Johnny Ringo, Charlton Heston as Henry Hooker, Jason Priestley as Billy Breckinridge
Video: Available on videocassette, laser disc, and DVD

TRUE LIES (1994)
20th Century–Fox

Director: James Cameron
Producer: James Cameron
Screenplay: James Cameron
Cinematography: Russell Carpenter
Musical score: Brad Fiedel
Principal cast: Arnold Schwarzenegger as Harry Tasker, Jamie Lee Curtis as Helen Tasker, Tom Arnold as Albert "Gib" Gibson, Bill Paxton as Simon, Tia Carrere as Juno Skinner, Art Malik as Salim Abu Aziz, Charlton Heston as Spencer Trilby
Video: Available on videocassette, laser disc, and DVD

IN THE MOUTH OF MADNESS (1995)
New Line Cinema

Director: John Carpenter
Producers: Michael De Luca and Sandy King
Screenplay: Michael De Luca
Cinematography: Gary B. Kibbe
Musical score: John Carpenter, Dave Davies, and Jim Lang
Principal cast: Sam Neill as John Trent, Jurgen Prochnow as Sutter Cane, Julie Carmen as Linda Styles, Charlton Heston as Jackson Harglow, Frances Bay as Mrs. Pickman
Video: Available on videocassette

ALASKA (1996)
CastleRock Entertainment/Columbia Pictures

Director: Fraser Clarke Heston
Producers: Andy Burg and Carol Fuchs
Screenplay: Scott Myers
Cinematography: Tony Westman
Musical score: Reg Powell
Principal cast: Thora Birch as Jessie Barnes, Vincent Kartheiser as Sean Barnes, Dirk Benedict as Jake Barnes, Charlton Heston as Perry, Duncan Fraser as Koontz
Video: Available on videocassette and laser disc

HAMLET (1996)
CastleRock Entertainment/ Turner/Columbia

Director: Kenneth Branagh
Producer: David Barron
Screenplay: Kenneth Branagh
Cinematography: Alex Thomson
Musical score: Patrick Doyle
Principal cast: Kenneth Branagh as Hamlet, Derek Jacobi as Claudius, Julie Christie as Gertrude, Kate Winslet as Ophelia, Richard Briers as Polonius, Brian Blessed as The Ghost, Charlton Heston as the Player King, Rufus Sewell as Fortinbras
Video: Available on videocassette and laser disc

GIDEON'S WEBB (1998)
Baldwin/Cohen Productions

Director: Claudia Hoover
Producer: Jack Gilardi, Jr.
Screenplay: Brad Mirman
Principal cast: Christopher Lambert as Gideon Webb, Charlton Heston as Addison Sinclair, Shirley Jones as Elly Morton, Carroll O'Connor as Leo Barnes, Mike Connors as Harland Greer
Video: Available on videocassette

Selected BIBLIOGRAPHY

Bazin, André. *Orson Welles: A Critical View.* New York: Harper & Row, 1978.

Comito, Terry. *Touch of Evil: Orson Welles, Director.* With contributions by François Truffaut, Howard Thompson, André Bazin, et al. New Brunswick, N.J.: Rutgers University Press, 1985.

Cornell, Katharine. *I Wanted to Be an Actress.* New York: Random House, 1939.

Crowther, Bruce. *Charlton Heston: The Epic Presence.* London: Columbus Books, 1977.

DeMille, Cecil B. *The Autobiography of Cecil B. DeMille,* ed. Donald Hayne. Englewood Cliffs, N.J.: Prentice Hall, 1959.

Dick, Bernard F. *Columbia Pictures: Portrait of a Studio.* Lexington, KY.: University Press of Kentucky, 1992.

Dickens, Homer. *The Films of Gary Cooper.* New York: Citadel Press, 1970.

Douglas, Kirk. *The Ragman's Son.* New York: Simon and Schuster, 1988.

Essoe, Gabe and Lee, Raymond. *DeMille: The Man and His Pictures.* New York: Castle Books, 1970.

Fine, Marshall. *Bloody Sam: The Life and Films of Sam Peckinpah.* New York: Donald I. Fine, 1991.

Freedland, Michael. *Gregory Peck.* New York: William Morrow, 1980.

Griggs, John. *The Films of Gregory Peck.* Secaucus, N.J.: The Citadel Press, 1984.

Herman, Jan. *A Talent for Trouble: The Life of Hollywood's Most Acclaimed Director, William Wyler.* New York: Putnam's, 1995.

Heston, Charlton. *In the Arena: An Autobiography.* New York: Simon & Schuster, 1995.

Heston, Charlton. *The Actor's Life: Journals 1956–1976,* ed. Hollis Alpert. New York: E. P. Dutton, 1976.

Higham, Charles. *Cecil B. DeMille.* New York: Charles Scribner's Sons, 1973.

Higham, Charles. *Orson Welles: The Rise and Fall of an American Genius.* New York: St. Martin's Press, 1985.

Higham, Charles and Hal Wallis. *Starmaker: The Autobiography of Hal Wallis.* New York: Macmillan, 1980.

Holden, Anthony. *Laurence Olivier.* New York: Atheneum, 1988.

Kim, Erwin. *Franklin J. Schaffner.* Metuchen, N.J.: The Scraecrow Press, 1985.

Leaming, Barbara. *Orson Welles.* New York: Viking Penguin, 1985.

Madsen, Axel. *The Authorized Biography of William Wyler.* New York: Crowell, 1973.

Malvern, Gladys. *Curtain Going Up! The Story of Katharine Cornell.* New York: Julian Messner, 1943.

Mierendorff, Marta. *William Dieterle: Der Plutarch von Hollywood, mit einer Studie von Jackie O'Dell.* Berlin: Henschel, 1993.

Missiaen, Jean-Claude. *Anthony Mann (Classiques du Cinéma).* Paris: Editions Universitaires, 1964.

Mosel, Tad and Gertrude Macy. *Leading Lady: The World and Theatre of Katharine Cornell.* Boston: Little, Brown, 1978.

Moss, Robert F. *The Films of Carol Reed.* New York: Columbia University Press, 1987.

Munn, Michael. *Charlton Heston: A Biography.* New York: St. Martin's Press, 1986.

Ringgold, Gene and DeWitt Bodeen. *The Films of Cecil B. DeMille.* New York, The Citadel Press, 1969.

Rovin, Jeff. *The Films of Charlton Heston.* Secaucus, N.J.: The Citadel Press, 1983 .

Sinyard, Neil. *The Films of Richard Lester.* Totowa, N.J.: Barnes & Noble Books, 1985.

Spoten, Donald. *Laurence Olivier: A Biography.* New York: Harper Collins, 1992.

Tuska, John. *The Filming of the West.* Garden City, N.Y.: Doubleday, 1976.

Wapshott, Nicholas. *The Man Between: A Biography of Carol Reed.* London: Chatto & Windus, 1990.

INDEX

(Page numbers in *italic* refer to illustrations.)

Photo CREDITS

DESIGNED BY

Susi Oberhelman

TYPEFACES IN THIS BOOK ARE

Electra, designed in 1935 by William Addison Dwiggins,
Helvetica Neue, a redraw of the Linotype Helveticas
of the early 1980s, and Bank Gothic

PRINTED AND BOUND BY

RR Donnelley & Sons Company

WAITERS
CHINESE RESTAURANT

EXIT

BAR — NEW HILTON

9/1

MOJAVE LOCATION